7 VEILS

MYSTICAL SECRETS OF A FEMININE PATH TO ENLIGHTENMENT

Dear Cornelia,
Your beautiful soul shines!
Your gifts will be your guide.
will see you in the 7 Veils!
Love, Meredith ♡

Meredith Zelman Narissi M.S., P.T.P.

BALBOA
PRESS

A DIVISION OF HAY HOUSE

Scriptures taken from the Holy Bible, New International Version®, NIV®. Copyright © 1973, 1978, 1984, 2011 by Biblica, Inc.™ Used by permission of Zondervan. All rights reserved worldwide. www.zondervan.com The "NIV" and "New International Version" are trademarks registered in the United States Patent and Trademark Office by Biblica, Inc.™

Balboa Press books may be ordered through booksellers or by contacting:

Balboa Press
A Division of Hay House
1663 Liberty Drive
Bloomington, IN 47403
www.balboapress.com
1 (877) 407-4847

Because of the dynamic nature of the Internet, any web addresses or links contained in this book may have changed since publication and may no longer be valid. The views expressed in this work are solely those of the author and do not necessarily reflect the views of the publisher, and the publisher hereby disclaims any responsibility for them.

The author of this book does not dispense medical advice or prescribe the use of any technique as a form of treatment for physical, emotional, or medical problems without the advice of a physician, either directly or indirectly. The intent of the author is only to offer information of a general nature to help you in your quest for emotional and spiritual well-being. In the event you use any of the information in this book for yourself, which is your constitutional right, the author and the publisher assume no responsibility for your actions.

Any people depicted in stock imagery provided by Thinkstock are models, and such images are being used for illustrative purposes only.
Certain stock imagery © Thinkstock.

Print information available on the last page.

ISBN: 978-1-5043-7949-6 (sc)
ISBN: 978-1-5043-7951-9 (hc)
ISBN: 978-1-5043-7950-2 (e)

Library of Congress Control Number: 2017906631

Balboa Press rev. date: 07/14/2017

Dedicated with Love to Quinn
...and to You Beloved Reader

TABLE OF CONTENTS

Acknowledgments ix
Introduction: Entrance to the 7 Veils................................xiii
Veils and Mystery, The Significance of Seven, Seven Wisdoms

Chapter 1: THE RED VEIL 1
The First Veil: The Red Veil of Denial

The Red Veil, My Story in the Red Veil, Veil of Denial, Little Girl, Repressed Expression, Remember, The Legacy of Divinity, Feminine Ways of Knowing, Innate knowing, Scheherazade, Seven Wisdoms, Experiential Dance Activities, Delusion and Illusion, More of My Story in the Red Veil

Chapter 2: THE ORANGE VEIL...............................21
The Second Veil: The Orange Veil of Sensation

The Ancient Dance, Veil of Sensation, Rejection of the Body, Her, The Goddess Within, Do Animals Dance?, Body Play, Jeanette by Jeanette Geraci, Control and Freedom, Seven Wisdoms, Experiential Dance Activities, My Story in The Orange Veil, Sensing Love and Fear, Stage Fright, Rebecca's Story by Rebecca Ness, Opening to Sensation

Chapter 3: THE YELLOW VEIL 47
The Third Veil: The Yellow Veil of Observation

Veil of Observation, Sunrise Dance, My Story in The Yellow Veil, Daughter of the Dancer by Lisa (my daughter: Michelle Spokes), Observing and Learning, Observation and Choice, Seven Wisdoms, Experiential Dance Activities, Who Am I?, Self- Observation, A Divine Glimpse...and a Story of Moses, Who Are You?, Kalae by Kalae Kaina, Observing your Life, Miriam by Miriam Groisman, Observation at the Beach, What is Arising?, Dance on

Chapter 4: THE GREEN VEIL 74
The Fourth Veil: The Green Veil of Love

Love Veil, 2 My Mother...Love, She Dances by Richard Ian Ries, Seven Wisdoms, Experiential Dance Activities, Holy Healing Dance, My Story in the Green Veil: A Highly Personal Story, Epilogue: The aftermath, The Dance of Love, the Dance of the Heart, Love Story, Give and Receive, Love is Natural, Become a Klutz, My "Second" Love Story, Love as Spiritual Practice, Love and Compassion, *The Lost Joy*, Sympathy, Forgiveness and Compassion

Chapter 5: THE BLUE VEIL..103
The Fifth Veil: The Blue Veil of Integration

Veil of Integration and Harmony, Morning Thoughts, Possibilities, Story of Nata by Nata Chantilly, The Not-So-Young, Not-So-Old Woman, Seven Wisdoms, Experiential Dance Activities, Masculine and Feminine Integration, Beauty and the Beast, Sadness Integrated, Dancing Through the Storm by Patty Maraldo, Self-Judgment and External Criticism, On Combating Negative Judgments about Belly Dancing, THEY & THEM, THIS & THAT By Dr. Ellen Haimoff, Confessions of a Soulfuldancer by Rosangel Perez, Adoring Eyes, Belly Dancing, and Parenting Your Inner Child, How to Adore, My Story in The Blue Veil: Curtains On Kirtan, Sisterhood and Belly Dancing, Dancing and Aging, My Thighs White, Aging into Softness, Menopause and More, Kismet's Dance, Integration and Mystery, Baruch Hashem

Chapter 6: THE PURPLE VEIL 145
The Sixth Veil: The Purple Veil of Promise

Seven Wisdoms, Experiential Dance Activities, Promise and Imagination, Perfection and Promise, My Story in the Purple Veil: Crazy Daze Vortex, Dance and Grace, Grace M.I.A., Imagination Required, My Teacher Dahlena, A Short Description of Dance and What it Means to Me by Dahlena, Wisdom and Promise

Chapter 7: THE WHITE VEIL..165
The Seventh Veil: The White Veil of Stillness

Oh the Dance By Davira Bareli, The Gifts of the River, Seven Wisdoms, Experiential Dance Activities, Learning, Natural Talents, and Practice, Seven Types of Intelligent Gifts, What is Enlightenment?, Distilled to the Essential, Clouds, The Edge, Music And, At the Still Point, Death of a Dance, My Story in the White Veil, Dance is ultimately a Godly pursuit, Abra Kedabra, The Veil of Stillness unveils Peace, Prayer-Body Birthing Dance, Holy Birth

Bibliography..191
Appendix 195

ACKNOWLEDGMENTS

A book is never just a one person endeavor. There are many people to thank.

I wish first and foremost to acknowledge my beloved, amazing, loving husband Stephen; for guiding me, for teaching me more about love than I taught him, for supporting me in so many ways, and for encouraging my creativity. And most of all, for loving me and letting me love him. I am so blessed to have him in my life.

Gratitude for my wise and loving children who also inspired and encouraged me, and who's superb talents far exceed mine. Their words and hearts are filled with love: Lisa (Michelle Spokes), Richard, and Arielle, and their loving spouses Brendan and Sebastien, and also to their gifts of our endearing grandchildren: Quinn, Liam, Juda, and Edie who help me see Divinity in their eyes, and in their questions. Especially to beautiful Quinn for her weekly loving visits and our super close bond. I quoted her more than anyone in this book!

A very special acknowledgement to my dear son Richard...Dr. Richard Ries, a psychologist who lives in Honolulu, who took many hours to lovingly correct and edit my work. His discerning view, his kind corrections, and the love we share is invaluable.

Gratitude and love to my beautiful daughter Lisa...Michelle Spokes, who led the very first meeting that birthed this book. She is a writer and yoga teacher and English teacher with extraordinary gifts of grace. I love her dearly.

A special thank you to Dr. Abigail Brenner for her mentoring and steadfast interest in my success. Her books were my inspiration, especially since she let me write a piece for one of her books about transformation! Please check out her work on Amazon: *Replacement Children: The unconscious script*, and *Women's Rite of Passage*. Her encouragement was a true gift that helped me move forward every step of the way. She lovingly and uncompromisingly motivated me to do my best.

Thank you to Babs Hogan, my helpful, loveable, loyal and kind Texas partner in writing. She is known on Facebook as "the healthy cheese lady." She has guided, and encouraged my book into being, as only a writer friend can. She spent much time and energy encouraging me and helping to edit my book. She is writing and blogging on the benefits of cheese as a healthy part of nutrition. Her new book *Say Cheese*, will be out soon.

To Bonnie Monchik my beloved confidant, meditation soul-sister, and dearest, insightful friend. It is such a blessing to have her in my life on this soulful level. She has been a great catalyst for my spiritual growth and I am deeply grateful always...beyond words.

And great thankfulness to all my sweet Dancing Divas who have inspired me while I teach them! Especially to the Divas and the one Divo who wrote for this book: Lisa...Michelle Spokes, Dr. Richard Ries, Dr. Ellen Haimoff, Miriam Groisman, Rebecca Ness, Janette Gercei, Kalae Kaina, Nata Chantilly, Patty Maraldo, Davira Barielli, April Rose, Roseangel Perez, Sharon Chinitz, and Dalhena Genova. Love and Gratitude also to the incredible dancers Chani, Shiri, Page, Sharon, Shani, Gina, Enid, Francine, Dara, Judea, Alexandra, and Miriam Grenberger, who is in class more than I because she subs for me! She, Rebecca and Chani have also helped to bring our dance to the stage.

Dr. Ellen, is my dear, sweet, psychologist friend who listens with her kind and loving ways, while I spout idea after idea, before I put them to the written word. Her input, wisdom, patience and love, are all profoundly guiding. And she is so much fun!

Gratitude to Jody LaGreca, who while swimming laps in the pool told me she was an author. Wonderful books...she gave me much guidance and editing too. Check out her author page.

Miriam Groisman for her dancing, and for the sweet generous and loving Saturdays with the "girls"..meaning her children and my granddaughter!

And my beloved friend Marilyn Roth, who I've loved since our youth, and who doesn't hold any view of me that isn't wonderful. I feel the same! She is like "perfection" in wisdom and kindness.

Thank you too to Mary Dale my intellectual, supportive, loving and insightful cousin; and to Penny Canamare, who really knows what it means to listen, especially as I was just beginning.

Ester Wein, an inspiration to so many with her gifted, awesome teachings, is even more astounding one-on-one. Profound gratitude to you, my sweet spiritual friend.

Thank you to the fabulous photographer Robert Bresnahan, we miss you, and to sweet creative Christine Santos, who also helped design the cover and took my author photo.

And of course to my dear incredible parents, Dr. Henry and Arline Zelman, who loved me, paid for dance lessons, believed in me, and gave me wonderfully supportive brothers and a sister to love after they were gone. Pamela Capone, my truest loving and loveable soul-sister ever, she always understands me...and to Doctors Russell and Warren Zelman, amazing, smart and loving brothers; all who share life and love with me in compassion and dedication. I am so blessed to have them in my life. We all share a deep love.

My teachers of dance; most notably Dahlena, who brought my gift to life with her careful, watchful eye, and amazing grace and love; thank you.

And to my readers: a book is only as good as the reader who appreciates it.

I offer my deepest gratitude and love to all.

INTRODUCTION

Entrance to the 7 Veils

"Kismet"

Veils and Mystery

Do you wish to be spellbound? Then contemplate the Seven Veils. Mystical secrets hide within them. You are enveloped in ethereal layers of protection and insight. Which one wraps around you now? Once you unveil, wisdom enters. It comes in enigmatic ways.

Natural veils, like mist, fog, and smoke, create a sense of the surreal. They evoke a notion of what lies beyond. You intuit shape or shadow, a sound here or there, an element of danger, or even beauty. When light pierces, you are caught between worlds. You watch the mundane restructure. You see visual evidence of the great mystery.

This profound unveiling happened for me through the art of belly dancing. Of course, you do not have to dance in order to reveal secrets of the veil, but it certainly helps. The body has memory. Ancient secrets awaken as you dance. From inside your cells, ancestral memory and instinctual nature shed insight into the present moment. Belly Dance is a practice that unveils.

Anthropologists suggest that belly dancing originated 5,000 to 25,000 years ago. Perhaps it was Eve's first dance. It has always involved celebration of the Feminine. Paradigms and archetypical images of womanhood: maiden, goddess, mother, and crone are highlighted. Womanly curves articulate round inclusive cycles of life. The dance movements express this: round as in pregnant, the shape of Mother Earth, a sacred circle where everyone sees everyone's eyes, and round like the arc of a flowing veil.

The origin of the dance involves fertility rites, harem choices, strengthening the body for childbirth, seduction to encourage a bride and groom to connect, the collection of coins for a dowry, sisterhood, and finally, for religious ecstasy. From art to entertainment, belly dance travels a wide artistic spectrum. It holds feminine elegance, self-control, and the freedom to embrace full womanhood. A natural feminine flowering, not always encouraged in our world, is a strong force. If not stopped or perverted, it becomes a journey into the psyche connecting all things.

It is a mistake to assume that the body is not spiritual. The split between natural and ephemeral, physical and spiritual, temporal and ultimate is actually a continuum. Ask any professional dancer, the art of dance is transcendent. There is rapture in dance. The artist and the creation cannot be separated. An author can read her words. A painter can view his painting. A musician can hear his instrument. Yet a dancer must *be* her dance. She cannot see it. It is like trying to look into your own eyes. She can, however, feel it, and therefore be one with it.

> *"Dance is the only art of which we ourselves*
> *are the stuff of which it is made..."*
> -Ted Shawn

This creative, spiritual dance is an initiation. This dance is medicine. It is a path of ecstasy where other spheres of understanding emerge. It symbolizes healing. This healing manifests through the seven veils.

It is easy to think of veils as a cover, more surprisingly as portals of insight. They hold imagination, the make-believe where you see truth in another form. You are persuaded then to see not only with the eyes, but with the soul. As you look into the veil, as well as into what is being revealed, layers of understanding emerge.

Veils of diaphanous material have lightness of matter. They hold at once substance and emptiness. They carry flowing energy that continues even after an initial impulse. Thus, veils have a dance all their own. Moving like water or air, they flow and fall in graceful rhythm. They seem alive. If you throw a veil into the air and let it land on its own, it will *never* float down in the same way twice. Seduction arises as a result of this unpredictability. Stories of veils and unveilings offer intrigue. You want to see what happens next. You want to know what comes to pass.

As each veil is met, in the seven veils of this book, wisdom will visit you. It appears when you are willing to receive. Each chapter invites you beyond a veil to reveal a mystical secret. These are furtive, deeply feminine ways of knowing that I have learned through the art of belly dancing. This antediluvian wisdom belongs to all of us. As I share each chapter, comparisons with other perceptive traditions will correlate to each of the seven veils.

The Significance of Seven

Perhaps every number has a list of noteworthy meanings, yet seven stands out as one of the most sacred numerals.

- There are seven days of creation in many traditions, and the seventh day is sanctified as the Sabbath.
- There are seven colors of the visible rainbow.
- There are seven seas and seven continents on our earth.
- In Galician folklore, a seventh son will be a werewolf. In other European folklores, the seventh son of a seventh son will be a child with special powers of healing and clairvoyant seeing.
- In ancient Greek lore, the number of gateways traversed by the goddess Inanna, during her descent into the underworld, is seven. She was said to have taken off seven articles of clothing by the end of her journey.
- In the Jewish tradition, there are seven universal moral codes in the Talmud called *The Seven Laws of Noah*. They are a sacred inheritance of all the children of Noah. And, at a Jewish wedding the bride traditionally walks around the groom seven times to honor that "a woman shall surround a man."
- In Hindu weddings the bride and groom walk around a holy fire seven times during the ceremony.
- In Islamic tradition during the rituals of Hajj, a pilgrimage to Mecca, pilgrims walk around the Kaaba seven times.
- There are seven Sacraments in Catholicism: seven ceremonies that point to what is most sacred.
- St. Teresa of Avila, a famed mystic, was inspired by her vision of the soul as a crystal castle containing seven mansions. She deciphered this as a journey of faith through seven stages.
- Shakespeare has eloquently written about the seven stages of man.

The list goes on. Surprisingly, when I asked myself what the mystical secrets of a feminine path toward enlightenment were, I too ended up with seven sacred answers.

Seven Wisdoms

You will see parallels as each veil is compared to other traditions. As I juxtaposed them, I was impressed with the acute overlay of concepts. This lent validation for my own precepts. What I wish to impart to you runs true with other valued paths of spirituality and enlightenment. They don't always coincide exactly, but if you follow the chain of evolvement, there are definite equivalents too similar to ignore. Eventually they dovetail into the same message of spiritual awakening.

Using the following wisdom insights or traditions, further understanding will come into view: Deepak Chopra's *Seven Laws of Spiritual Success*, The Seven Stages of Development for a Yogi Before Achieving Complete Liberation, The Seven Chakras, Lawrence Kohlberg's Stages of Moral Development, Buddhism's Seven Factors of Enlightenment, and finally, the seven tasks of love enumerated in the story of *The Skeleton Woman*: *Facing the Life/Death/Life Nature of Love*, as referenced in one of my most favorite books, *Women who Run with the Wolves: Myths and Stories of the Wild Woman Archetype,* by Clarissa Pinkola Estes, Ph.D. She is a well known Jungian psychoanalyst and writer.

Stories of my personal journey with belly dancing, and other dancers' tales of transformation also shed light on this path. These dancers have contributed narratives by opening their hearts to you. Each one explores how the dance has changed her life. Liberation from social phobia, release from a difficult marriage, drug abuse, freedom, overcoming negative views, coming out of a cult, or just wanting more love, are some of the themes explored. Sprinkle in a poem here and there, along with inspiring quotes, and you will move from one veil to another, ever illuminating deeper mystical secrets.

Healing has manifested for me through my dance within these seven veils. As you process in your own creative way, your dance through the veils will be the only one of its kind. This migration is a template, not a prescription. Yet in my work as a mind/body polarity therapist, it has been helpful for me to use the veils as a marker for my clients spiritual development. Where are you in the work of the veils? As you read on, you may want to ask which veil is relevant to you at this time. Which veil would you be unveiling next?

Each veil suggests an *experiential dance activity*. Please feel free to play, dance, and open to each unveiling. The dance activities are non-verbal explorations of healing. You can do many by yourself, yet others require a partner or a group. Free the mind and learn from the body. Let the unconscious gifts of creativity be brought to the light. The explorations are meant to emancipate you, and therefore must be done in *sacred space*. This means that you dance from the heart, watch others dance with your heart, and ask for Divine presence. There is no judgment during this creative stage of sacred space. Each activity is only a suggestion, so follow the requirements of your own body and mind. Also, most importantly, enjoy yourself!

As an artful dancer unwraps her gossamer veil revealing beauty, I wish *your* secrets to become unveiled. As you read on, may the genuine beauty of your true nature be revealed. It is my hope that you are inspired to deepen your path toward enlightenment. Let the pain and suffering life brings you be eased through change. Healing creates a dwelling place of knowing peace, loving-kindness, and joy. Even when we are not in that space, we hold the knowledge of it. That is what I wish for you.

Dancing through the gifts of belly dancing, I have traveled from student to performer to teacher, from presenter, speaker-writer, to polarity therapist and spiritual healer. As a *mystagogue,* a person whose teachings are founded on mystical revelation, and one who initiates others into the sacred mysteries, I offer the gifts I have received along the way, and pass them forward. Open your mind and heart. Let the words dance around you until you feel their meaning. Let your inner wisdom flow with the muses. Awaken now and come dance with me. Dance with me through the veils! We are all on this journey together. See the veil? Please enter.

CHAPTER 1

THE RED VEIL

The First Veil: The Red Veil of Denial

Red Veil of Denial

I was in denial. Before I became the swan, before I truly understood the secrets of a feminine path to enlightenment, I was in a state of illusion. I was pretending for a long time, entwined in red gossamer fabric.

The Red Veil

The veil of denial is velvety red, blood red. It trails behind you with a train so long, you're not sure where it ends, or where it begins. Its color is flame streaked, sanguine, and sometimes stoplight red. In a legacy of bloodlines, it wraps around you tightly several times. A gossamer elegance drapes the shape of your body in a snake's embrace. This snake is a healing snake, not a sinful snake. It is one of fear and courage, both asleep and awake. The over-layered binding of this veil feels rooted and secure, but you also feel stuck.

This veil holds potent survival knowledge. Like a seed buried deep within red earthen ground, it stretches out its roots for nutrients and forthcoming sunlight; something stirs, something is moving. A vague yearning rouses. Desire achingly calls your hands to unravel this tight veil. Under yards and yards of vermilion, there are miles and miles of time and ancient ancestry striving to push you toward the light. You wish to unveil.

My Story in the Red Veil

The dance came, like a gift. I wasn't seeking it. The place where I lived, with my husband and two children, had a clubhouse where special events were held. The sign on the activity room door said "Belly Dancing." Twenty people had to sign up before the two teachers would come to instruct a class. I love to dance and did not have a car at the time, so this seemed perfect. A dance studio had come to me. I recruited friends and neighbors, and we finally had a class. Sadly, I do not recall my first teachers' names. In the light of the amazing master teachers to follow, they remain a dim, yet sweet memory. What stays with me most is their enthusiastic belief in my abilities.

There was to be a big contest for *the best belly dancer*, and all the dance schools were eager to enter their finest students. As a beginner, I had not considered myself eligible. Amazingly, my instructor's offered to send a different teacher to my house each week, free of charge, to prepare me for the contest! It was the classic example of opportunity knocking on the door. So, I said, "Yes." A life changing "Yes!" I opened the door...or was it a Veil?

Famous George Abdo would be singing along with his talented band, and the judges were all well-known dancers. Excited and nervous, I practiced ardently. I even invested in a handmade costume. The woman who made the costume also offered me a lesson. I gladly accepted. It seemed that support was coming from everywhere. My children and neighbors became accustomed to the sweet strains of Middle Eastern music and the offbeat clattering of my zills— finger symbols, which I could not master in the few weeks of preparation.

On the day of the contest, my husband, always encouraging my creativity, reserved a table of supportive friends for my on-stage debut. Although I was appreciative, I soon felt captive in an ordeal involving some rite of passage! As I watched each enchanted, shimmering, vision dancing before me, I was certain each one was a lot better than me! After all, I had only taken about sixteen classes and a few private sessions.

Surprisingly, when my turn came, performance jitters melted in the spotlight. I knew this dance! Could it be from a previous lifetime, my Greek and Semitic roots, some deep archetypical Goddess living in my psyche? Perhaps it reflected my longing to share my elemental being. When I danced on stage that night, it felt like being home. I was remembering ancient haunting music. I was remembering the dance. It felt like the dance and I were One.

My photo went into the newspaper and I could not believe I had actually won! One of the judges, Vena, offered to give me private lessons. I said "Yes" again. The dance found me, and yet it seemed somehow that I had been seeking it.

Juxtaposed with challenges in my marriage, where rose colored glasses finally fell to the floor and shattered, the dance became my saving grace—literally. When my lovability was in question, I could be adored on stage. When my sexuality was not enough, I was superlatively seductive. When my self-esteem could not hold all I needed, my alter-ego expanded. This dance can heal.

These were my early understandings of the dance. We would continue to evolve together. At this time, I was exceedingly unhappy and unaware. I thought I could outsmart the unprincipled choices offered. It seemed that I could ignore the felt-sense that something wasn't quite right. I needed to see more clearly. I was in denial, as in Queen of De-Nile. Those rose colored glasses were quite polished and protective. But, I had my dancing. That's where I was the Queen, De-Nile or not. It felt good for the time being. So I clung to it as an identity. I clung to it for the survival of my psyche.

Veil of Denial

The red veil flaunts a denial that you need to recognize. Denial occurs when you choose to be unaware. You choose, consciously or unconsciously, or else you could not "deny." It appears to be a favorite defense mechanism. You want to avoid pain and suffering. There may be trauma you don't wish to recall, or some experience that could cause you regret. Denial lives in a world of illusion. You dabble in denial. Take death for instance. You most likely think about it happening to someone else—not you! There is an interesting Buddhist chant that says "I will get old, I will get sick, and I will die." That's not exactly in alignment with current trends of positive thinking, but it sure is a denial buster! In inimitable Buddhist style, it can remind you of impermanence, thus bringing you back to enjoy the life you now have. As you discover and embrace being with your denial and resistance, yearning invariably awakens. This yearning shows what can be possible.

Little Girl

Once upon a time there was a timid little girl who was also brave. She liked to play street games and be the leader, yet at school she was shy and sensitive. Did you know her? Were you like her? She was smart and insightful but careful. It made her afraid to make mistakes. Her favorite fairy tale was "The Ugly Duckling."

She was in the slow reading group and not one of the popular kids. She didn't know she was smart or pretty, yet she liked to pretend she was. She held a great love of family, friends, and life. Her turbulent journey took her through trials and tribulations, as it does for all of us.

She often saw great birds flying overhead and wondered about their magnificence. They seemed to be calling her. Their call held a profound mysterious longing. Her thoughts went back and forth. She assumed that the swans had nothing to do with her. And then, she would think, in some way, she was just like them. What was she missing?

Her head turned when they came by, her ears listened, and her eyes scanned their beauty. She loved to watch them fly through the crimson veiled sunset along the horizon. She came to know them in this way. By and by, many discoveries came to her, yet in her distraction, she lost touch with the swans. She found love, enjoyed learning, earned accolades, raised a family, and created her legacy. Along the way, she learned to love herself. That meant forgiving herself. It was one of the sweetest, wisest, and hardest lessons to learn, like learning to fly. She noticed that she was beginning to change. She was beginning to see beyond illusive coverings. She remembered the swans.

Mystical secrets were always waiting in the background for her swan likeness to emerge, and so it happened. This swan was not the great bird of *Swan Lake*, it was instead a rare, strange bird of exotic elegance. Her transformation flew to her, carrying secrets. She learned because she was used to transcending. She transcended through the art of belly dance. She transcended through the veils. And so it was.

Repressed Expression

The first veil is repressed expression calling. You sense something thwarting your creativity. Like the little girl, you are not sure where you belong. If you see past resistance, you find the seed of something you long to know.

You watch a belly dancer. You think, *I can't dance, don't ask me.* Then you think, *But this dance does look alluring, maybe I can do it.* Dormant longings revive a great craving. *I have this Belly Dance somewhere within me.* Desire for the deep feminine flame has just been lit.

What is behind this veil of denial? You can ask yourself to pause here and see the red veil more clearly. Why do you want to avoid seeing through it? Does it offer protection for awhile? Peek under and around your veil. What do you see? What is it that you want? What is it that you *deny* yourself?

After a time, curiosity arises. You want to explore deep feminine knowing. Desire can move avoidance. Or does the veil remain stoic and steadfast in its place? Be patient. Remember a time in your life when you faced denial. Was there ultimately a heartfelt gift that emerged? Was it something you aspired to that actually came true?

Become entranced by this veiled desire. It is your desire for the expression you have repressed. You can explore ways for it to be revealed. You may want to practice an embellished visualization rich in possibilities. This is a kind of prayer. See yourself being the dancer. See yourself actualizing the dream. Look beyond. You are the seed of the blossom. You are the beauty behind the veil. From somewhere, you remember this dance.

Remember

There is a hazy ambiguity about belly dance that one unravels only after many years of practice. It is similar to a nagging afterthought, like something you forgot. Maybe it's a vague dream upon awakening that hovers at the edge of consciousness. Or it is like a taste on the tip of your tongue, a sweet honey remembrance, as you try to recall a recipe. This evocative jogging of your memory makes you want the recipe, the taste, and the whole dream with meaning and analysis. Be curious. What is so ephemeral and distant?

Then, out of the body-knowing comes a familiar reverie. Sensual and ancestral awareness awakens. You talk about it in quotation marks, yet it strikes a primal chord of truth. It is the feminine face of God: the Shekhinah, Astra, Isis, Pele, Mary, and all the mother, birthing, creatrix symbols. Not in just a metaphoric way, but in the way of Goddess worship. Not in polite afterthoughts to appease a forgotten power, but in the way of reverence. It has a long legacy like the train of the red veil trailing behind you. You have missed something long denied. Perhaps the veil of denial hides your desire for Divine connection. Do you deny God?

The Legacy of Divinity

As quoted from *Goddesses in Everywoman*, chapter 1, Jean Shinoda Bolen, M.D., author and Jungian psychiatrist, notes that there is an unspoken history. Harper Collins Publishing:

(Dating back over 5000 to perhaps 25,000 years)

Old Europe was a matrifocal, sedentary, peaceful, art-loving, earth and sea bound culture that worshipped the Great Goddess. Evidence gleaned from burial sites show that Old Europe was an unstratified, egalitarian society that was destroyed by an infiltration of semi nomadic, horse-riding, Indo-European peoples from the distant north and east. These invaders were patrifocal, mobile, warlike, ideologically sky-oriented, and indifferent to art.

The invaders viewed themselves as a superior people because of their ability to conquer the more culturally developed earlier settlers, who worshipped the Great Goddess. Known by many names- Astarte, Ishtar, Inanna, Nut, Isis, Ashtoreth, Au Set, Hathor, Nina, Nammu, and Nigal, among others- the Great Goddess was worshipped as the feminine life force deeply connected to nature and fertility, responsible both for creating life and for destroying life. The snake, the dove, the tree, and the moon were her sacred symbols.

According to historian-mythologist Robert Graves, before the coming of patriarchal religions the Great Goddess was regarded as immortal, changeless, and omnipotent.

Successive waves of invasions by the indo-Europeans began the dethronement of the Great Goddess. …The goddesses were not completely suppressed, but were incorporated into the religion of the invaders."

This remembrance illustrates one of our greatest collective denials: our forgetfulness of the Goddess within. To see the attributes of Divinity as only masculine cuts women off from their Divine knowing. Most religions and wisdom traditions remind us to look within to find the Divine spark of Divinity. When you think of God as only a *He*, being a woman can become an obstacle to igniting this spark. It's not as if you are going to find a Michelangelo God image living in your heart. I suppose even that's possible since God comes in all forms. Yet you are now giving God limits. Beyond idolatry there is also a feminine expression of Divine love. Even innocent children know this.

At a restaurant, in celebration of my daughter Lisa Michelle's birthday, the family was gathered to enjoy artful décor, exotic paintings, the melodic resonance of Eastern music, and deliciously spiced Indian cuisine. We chose Indian food in honor of her being a yoga teacher. I mentioned to my granddaughter that the taste of Indian food is like fireworks going off in your mouth. That did not exactly persuade her to try the strange-looking fare. She did, however, enjoy looking at the beautiful images of dancing women in the paintings. Then she was waving her hands and shifting her body to the lovely music— enough to get kind smiles from the Indian people watching her. After her attention came back to her mother and the birthday celebration, she asked me the following question. "Since you are my mother's mother, who was the first mother?"

This *first* mother is embodied in you. This feminine love is embedded within you, and also in Middle Eastern dance— another name for belly dancing. It carries the potent power of creation. Not only in artistic expression, but also in the imitation of birth. It imitates the bringing forth of life: our life, your life. It celebrates that you are here, and also how you got here. All of us got here through the body of the Goddess. Yes, as a woman, you were once worshiped for this. Remember that now. Secretly, you still are. The red veil of denial has kept you from your holy nature. But you can feel it when you perform. You can feel it when you belly dance. You can feel it when you remove the veils.

Feminine Ways of Knowing

Did you ever notice that the word feminine contains the word *in* twice? It doubles the letters *in*. Perhaps this emulates how a woman comes to know her body and her psyche. The feminine way of mysticism goes deeply inward. It implies awareness of the interior. I remember a psychology experiment where boys put toys outside a doll house while the girls put the toys inside. Having a women's body calls you *in* with very evident expression. Growing breasts, menstruation, pregnant bellies, and menopause speak loudly of internal change. Moon cycles, milk cycles, and birthing, are all powerful shifts. The birth of a baby from your body is astonishing— a personal miracle! These manifestations encourage embodied introspection. A pregnant woman may think, *How can this awe and metamorphosis be happening inside of me?*

When the Universe borrows your body to bring forth life, you feel it passing through. You know something of this great cosmic life force in an intimate way. Belly dancing personifies this. The undulations and belly movements imitate childbirth. Belly dance celebrates and awakens the hidden consciousness of the birthing Goddess.

When a male gives the essence, the spiritual essence, a woman brings it into matter, real being. Matter, originally called mater, shares a history with the word mother. Not every woman engages in birth matter. Some engage birth as spirit. When you give birth on a spirit level, something of mothering flowers from your feminine chromosomes. It is a privilege to be feminine and know the inner workings of creation from such a view. Whenever you are creative, you are practicing spiritual birthing and piercing the red veil. Before that it may be hidden.

Innate knowing

There is an angelic story about innate knowledge being hidden. It is an ancient folktale kept alive by oral tradition. It is the story of Lailah, the angel of conception. She brings the soul and the seed together, and is seen as an angelic midwife. She teaches the unborn child the holy scripture, and the story of its soul. When birth comes, she places her finger to the mouth of the child as if to say *sh,* and this causes the child to forget everything learned in the womb. That is why you have an indentation above your upper lip. It is called the philtrum.

Her name, Lailah, in Hebrew means night. It is a feminine name. There are not too many feminine angel names. The Greek word for angel in the New Testament is *Angelos*. It is in the masculine form. Today many statues and pictures of feminine angels abound. These angelic creatures usually reflect the sweet virgin, or the loving mother imbued with feminine love. There is of course a counter-angel. We don't usually see her on the shelf! She represents the other side of the feminine.

While Lailah is nurturing, the myth of Lilith portrays a decidedly destructive kind of power. While Lailah protects the unborn child, Lilith seeks to destroy infants. Lilith was said to have been created in similar fashion to Adam, but not from his rib. She refused to be submissive and was said to prefer being on top. Having wandered in defiance from Adam, and Eden, she becomes a symbol of chaos and dark things of the night. She represents the shadow side. The red veil holds her close to your psyche as well. Removing the veil does not always imply seeing beauty. You will also see the shadow side. You must see it all.

These stories of Lailah and Lilith suggest that prevailing (no pun intended) knowledge exists within you, even if it is temporarily forgotten. How to remember involves intuition. If you cut yourself off from intuition, yes, that most famous "women's intuition," then denial rules. To rediscover your instinctual nature requires exploration of the self and finding your sixth sense. What self understanding do you avoid? Do you tell yourself the truth about your natural abilities?

There are clues from your childhood. What are your inborn gifts? How were they perceived by others? Do you know what they are? I have heard women say that they have no gifts. One woman told me her mother always said it was a good thing she was a nice girl, because she had no special talents. Quite unlikely. Even being nice *is* a talent!

I was fortunate that my mother lovingly told me stories of my creativity. She was a wonderful story teller, and we loved to sit around the table and listen to her enchanting tales. They often included stories about us! She said that when I was only three or four, I danced in the aisles of restaurants whenever the music inspired me. Luckily she found it charming. I started dance lessons when I was five, and then continued nonstop from the time I was eleven years old. I even enjoyed learning in forthcoming years. My parents supported my dance classes from the time I was young. They understood my natural gifts.

Parental generosity aside, I inherited gifts through legacy, as have you. A peculiar synchronicity occurred as well, as if to point out more clearly what destiny ordained. When I was an infant, my parents used to play music to soothe me to sleep. They played Scheherazade: a lyrical, exciting symphonic suite composed by Nikolai Rimsky-Korsakov based on *One Thousand and One Nights*...Arabian *belly dancing* nights! Scheherazade survived because of her storytelling gifts. The legend goes as such:

Scheherazade

Once there was a king who, betrayed by his unfaithful wife, acted out his anger by marrying virgins, only to have them beheaded the very next day! When Scheherazade, a lovely maiden, was asked to become his next wife, she devised a survival plan. Under the pretense of missing her sister, Scheherazade begged to have her come along. She then cleverly asked her sister to request a nightly story for the king. As Scheherazade kept the king in suspense by stopping in the middle of each story she told, she left each tale unfinished at the end of the night. She repeated this abrupt pause within each new narrative by proclaiming that dawn was breaking. As the king listened eagerly to Scheherazade's cliff hanging episodes, which would never be completed until the next night, he was compelled to allow yet another night of storytelling to follow...and yet another! Some of the stories include *Aladdin's Wonderful Lamp, Ali Baba and the Forty Thieves*, and *The Seven Voyages of Sinbad the Sailor*. This went on for 1001 nights. The King was now fascinated and charmed by Scheherazade. Having been made a wiser and kinder man by listening to her tales, he fell in love, spared her life, and happily made her his Queen.

The 1001 nights is a story from Persian culture, thought by many to be the birthplace of belly dancing. Perhaps as an infant, while listening to this beautiful music, I was dreaming of becoming a belly dancer. Apart from synchronicity, what called me to this music, this story, this dance? Could it be innate predispositions of DNA, inherited knowledge, or offerings of destiny? What was my knowing before the angel put "sh" to my lips?

At this red veil stage, just to acknowledge your talents, and to be honestly open to your inner knowing, is a grand step. Admitting that denial might be at work is wonderful. As you dance with the red veil, repression morphs into potentiality. What you fear holds secrets about what you want. Curiosity is engaged. Be curious about what holds you back.

Just as Scheherazade's gifts saved her life, your inborn gifts save your psychic life. As you come to know your personal aptitudes, your spirituality will be revealed to you. Embracing innate abilities leads you forward. Spirituality is unveiled in the practice of your talents. It is one step toward spirit as you remove the red veil of denial.

Seven Wisdoms

As you will see, all seven principles imply *awareness* of denial at this level. There is the suggestion to be silent in order to witness. Listen to find this awareness. Here is how the other seven insights and traditions name this denial.

- In *Deepak Chopra's Seven Spiritual Laws of Success: A practical Guide to the Fulfillment of Your Dreams*, he lists the first law:

  The Law of Pure Potentiality: be silent.

  Deepak reminds you that in silence denial becomes exposed. Potentials are revealed as you listen. It is interesting to note that dance can be silent.

- In *The Yogi's Seven Stages of Development before Achieving Complete Liberation,* it is stated this way:

  Stage 1: That which is to be known is known by me.

At this stage the yogi realizes that all
true knowledge comes from within oneself.

Here, being silent in order to find your pure potentiality is suggested again. First you will meet denial.

• In the *Seven chakras the first is Muladhara, the root chakra.*

The Sanskrit word Chakra literally means wheel or spinning disk. Chakras align with the spine, starting from the base of the spine to the crown of the head. Each represents an energy place where physicality and spirituality meet, where energy and consciousness meet. The chakras are used in many healing modalities.

This first root chakra, located at the perineal floor near the
base of the spine, deals with survival. It also deals with the
right to exist. It encompasses tasks related to the physical
world and a kind of earthy stability. It represents the earth
element. This energy at the base of the spine is related to
instinct, security, relationship to your tribe, and also to
basic human potentiality. It conveys courage and fear, and
the first seven years of life. It is noted as the color red.

Here, as you notice your fear and courage, it loosens this red veil of denial. Becoming aware of your survival instincts, you are now on the path of awakening. Fear can create denial, and courage can release it.

• In *Lawrence Kohlberg's Stages of Moral Development, Stage 1:*

Obedience and punishment orientation...
Egocentric deference to superior power or
prestige, or a trouble-avoiding set.

This orientation of reasoning is again survival mode. It is also about fear. An everyday example might be the desire of a child to steal cookies. They perceive that as long as they don't get caught, they are ok. If an adult reasons at that same level, and she measures what is right by what is at risk, it *denies* results. It obscures how her actions might affect or hurt others.

- Dr. Clarissa Pinkola Estes discusses *stages of love* in her chapter *The Skeleton Woman: Facing the Life/Death/Life Nature of Love.*

The first stage of love: The accidental finding of treasure
...discovering another person as a
kind of spiritual treasure.

Referenced in *Women who Run with the Wolves: Myths and Stories of the Wild Woman Archetype,* the Skeleton Woman story involves a man fishing innocently in a place considered taboo and haunted. He then strangely catches a skeleton woman instead of a fish! He can't seem to get rid of her. How he comes to learn of her story and how he relates to her is paramount.

Dr. Clarissa's first stage of love, illustrates finding love of another as a spiritual treasure. The story highlights the *skeleton* you find when looking at your loved one. You see the *not so beautiful* in them as well as in yourself. When you remove denial, perspective gains clarity. A wider perspective illuminates possibilities. You see the beautiful, and the not so beautiful. As denial falls away, you begin to allow spiritual treasures to emerge. You might even find the treasure of yourself. What treasure hides behind your veil?

- In *Buddhism's Seven Factors of Enlightenment,* the first stage is:

Mindfulness - Sati, which is to recognize
phenomena, or reality, with mindfulness.

This implies removing denial through acute awareness. Awareness of how the mind functions, as well as what the mind is thinking. Studying how and why you think, and the manner in which you think, loosens the red veil. All these ways of knowing support the notion that denial can be an ally toward enlightenment and healing.

• **The First Mystical Secret of The Red Veil of Denial**

Denial Unveils Desire

Denial is the first stage in healing the soul. At first you don't want to see that healing is required. You don't even want to know that you've been hurt. What occurs here is the telling of truth to yourself. You begin to let go of illusion. As you remove the veil of denial you discover a strong hidden undercurrent.

Call it desire, curiosity, or yearning. You find what I refer to as *The Big Cry*. It is running in your nervous system begging to be recognized. It can generate a reorganization of thoughts. It can help in the loss of bad habits. It can raise an awareness of spirit in matter, and all manner of avenues toward Divine Knowing. This is *The Big Cry* because you feel separate. We all feel separate. The parting of the veil of denial shows you the desire to connect: to connect with that which is holy.

Experiential Dance Activity:

o *Volcano Dance:* Pretend you are belly dancing on a volcano. Your feet are "stuck" to the floor. You might think the whole earth is shaking like this volcano, perhaps you are stuck in one place, one thought, one time. Can you dance from here?
o *Dance like the "Queen of De-nial:"* the queen of denial is also the queen of delusion, illusion, and fantasy. Finally, it holds the suggestion of what is possible.
o *Awaken the Sleeping Goddess*: one dancer is "asleep" and the other awakens her with a dance. Unveil someone and dance

with them. Then let them awaken your sleeping Goddess. She is within you, and you can help another awaken her sleeping beauty as well.

o *Dance In A Bubble of Space*: your highest, lowest, left, right, front, back, parameters of the bubble are reached as you move. Feel the confines of your limited movements and see if you can increase the space around them. For example can you reach higher if you jump?

o *Dance Tribal Circles* around each other. As a tribe you can help one another come out of the sleep of denial.

o *Cocoon Butterfly Veil Dance*: wrap yourself in a veil tightly. Imagine you are in a cocoon. The cocoon is a time for gestation of what is to come. Feel the flow of that change as you dance and free yourself to become the butterfly.

Delusion and Illusion

Death is, of course, one of the greatest concepts we deny. Yet if you imagine being very old, accumulating aliments over time, and finding it difficult to go on living, perhaps a desire for death would be an appropriate path to transformation. Our society holds a communal denial around this topic, yet there is awakening happening even on this frontier.

You use denial for avoidance. When you have trouble in a relationship, and the situation becomes unbearable, you use denial to stay. This covers up your need for a real and better relationship. Whether or not that includes the same person, or a wish to move on, the beating of your heart wants true love. Fear allows denial to stay in place until you part the veils. Sometimes it is the relationship with yourself that requires the mending. When you discern this need, illusion shifts, and new beginnings happen.

More of My Story in the Red Veil

I knew men found me attractive. I used to say, "I can make any man fall in love with me for five minutes if I belly dance." What I didn't want to know was that superficial love only lasts that symbolic five minutes! What I also didn't wish to see, was that this dance can evoke twists, wrong turns, and shiny mirages. It can lead to blind pathways. Especially when viewed behind a thick red veil.

Wrapped in red, the development of my egoic-woman felt like riding a great stallion at full speed. Feeling wind in my hair, exhilarated with athletic strength, flexibility and vulnerability, it became a whirling-dervish, non-stoppable trance. Where it would take me I was not sure, nor did I seem to care. Dancing in night clubs, even though I had never been in one before, and parties, while also performing in a dance company, combined entertainment and art. I was gaining expertise, deep love of the dance, and great joy in dancing. Yet my refusal to see beyond the veil persisted. This denial led to some belly dancing on the dark side.

"Behind the Veils"

"She is like a cat in the dark
And then she is the darkness
She rules her life like a fine skylark
And when the sky is starless

All your life you've never seen a woman
Taken by the wind
Would you stay if she promised you heaven?
Will you ever win?"

- Stevie Nicks, Best of Fleetwood Mac-Easy Piano

When I called my dance teacher Dahlena and asked her to write a piece for this book, she said, "You know, someone once asked me to write about the dark side of belly dancing, have you considered that?"

"Of course," I replied, "But I don't want to." Denial alert! She then cited stories of dancers who took drugs, committed suicide, or found themselves on a suffering path instead of one of ecstasy. My reluctance to write about the dark side was to avoid pain and suffering. Truly what brought me to the dance was as much from sadness as from happiness. Yes, the teachers had come to the clubhouse where I lived, and it was a serendipitous joining of events. But, there was a more sinister yeaning at play. One not only about creative expression but also of desperation. I was wounded and I did not want to know it.

The murky side of belly dancing invites you to believe that the image *is* you. You see the icon not the person, the representation not the woman. You become the lover who is not being loved for herself, but for her ego. You can entice men by portraying an alluring and irresistible role, yet still not understand why you feel so lonely.

This loneliness became obvious to me. I remember being at a pool one sunny day, wearing a yellow string bikini. My body felt luxurious in the warmth of the sun. Toned, tan and in great shape from belly dancing, the comfort of my body was in sharp contrast to the sadness of my heart. There, I felt alone and abandoned. As I watched two men adoring and hugging their not so attractive women, I realized that I had not experienced connection like that in quite some time. The discomfort was an awakening. I understood that no matter how beautiful, sexy, or attractive I was on stage, or in a bikini, love was not about that! Trying to trick someone into loving you, using intrigue and beauty, is not the same as being loved for who you are. By playing a role, you are removed from being your true self.

Play acting the feminine goddess *is* part of the journey toward finding your authentic self, but becoming too attached is not! The search for your essential self must prevail. Desperation and trying to be loved is not the same as being loving. Yet each stage is essential. The caterpillar does not become the butterfly without first becoming the cocoon. Even the struggle of leaving the cocoon provides power to the emerging butterfly. It strengthens the wings for flight.

Curiously, when I took modern dance in college, one of my first assignments was to choreograph a dance about a different life form. I chose a butterfly. I was painfully shy about coming out of my cocoon. In this new guise, I could grow wings and escape my encasement of fear. My mindset had been all about judgment. I was concerned about others liking, or not liking, what I was doing. It felt stuck. When I became the butterfly, I touched liberation. My inner wisdom was *dancing* exactly what I needed to know. My hidden knowledge presented the butterfly idea. It offered just the right medicine for my soul. Now when I dance from silky folded wings, I unveil and take pleasure in all of my beauty. This process took time. That inner knowing was breaking through denial.

If you are only feeling free on stage, you cannot know if you are loved for yourself or your persona. I was only the liberated butterfly on stage. Feeling unloved in my marriage, my loneliness continued. I had not learned to integrate the butterfly into the rest of my life.

When the wounded-self directs action, chaos surely follows. If you dabble on the dark side, you will know it soon enough. You make compromises where there should be boundaries. You rationalize and pretend. You avoid the here and now. You allow yourself to stay scared and pushed around by more and more wanting, until you lose sight of what is important.

Wanting is a form of suffering. You are then snaked in the red veil. This can happen in any form: money, drugs, alcohol, sex, work, or even the arts. It could even be those cookies in Lawrence Kohlberg's stage one. Cravings control your choices, and hunger and thirst are not satisfied...because you are entangled.

Feel the red veil and breathe. Slowly untwine the layers of silky fabric. Breathe again, something is shifting. Denial shifts to desire. What awakens within desire is not just a substitute for relinquishing illusion, but a true sense of feeling all that exists in the present moment. You begin to welcome sensation.

Ah, but I get ahead of myself...the rest of the story will require another veil. See the light shining beyond the red veil? Go toward it.

CHAPTER 2

⧼⧽

THE ORANGE VEIL

The Second Veil: The Orange Veil of Sensation

This orange veil is the color of a glorious sunrise and its subsequent sunset. Comings and goings of the sun epitomize attachment and loss. You watch the warm light fade away, only to return the next day. In shades of crocus-saffron, bright carrot, happy pumpkin, to burnt ochre, the orange veil flows unbounded. Invoking images of autumn leaves floating back and forth in a rock-a-bye-baby cascade, it makes the cradle of your hips want to sway.

The veil changes, rising and falling like a deep breath all the way down to your lower belly. As you breathe, you feel the orange veil slide across your torso with a silky brush of contact. It caresses and teases your nipples, awakening stirrings in deeper places. The veil's fluttering is reminiscent of internal contractions. You are bathed in a warm glow. Glittering sunbeams captivate your senses...all your senses...you revive and awaken here. You come alive. This orange veil touches your abdomen below the navel, the place of the hidden womb. The place you once lived in your mother. It is a sacred space. You were born from here.

This veil symbolizes awakening to your body. How to flow with this body-celebrating veil is the challenge. What is under this sensual awakening? What do you feel? Can the five senses lead you to a sixth sense? Is it safe to feel this much? Feeling pleasure and pain, ecstasy and suffering, and anguish to bliss, what mystical secret does this veil hold for you? Take a moment now to notice how much you feel your body, your breath, your sensory world. Consider how sensitive you are to feeling your body. What do you see, hear, taste, touch and smell in this moment? What are your feelings about your body? Do you experience it as an object to be viewed, or as a vehicle for sensing and experiencing life?

I have asked my yoga and dance students, "How did you feel about your body when you were 5 or 6 years old? Do you remember feeling your body?" Most of them replied that they weren't exactly aware of having a body.

Perhaps they were in tune with what yoga and polarity therapy calls the *energetic body*. In Polarity we understand the body as a field of energy. Maybe children feel more like *energy* than *body*. That is the state dancing can create— no physical or mental entrapments, just pure sensation. Uncensored sensation plays with energy. We all dance within these sensory inputs. In belly dancing, for a time, you become feminine energy, the wild instinctual woman immersed in sensation.

The Ancient Dance

She arcs eyeliner above watchful pupils and scans her face for transformation. The lipstick, the blush, and the eye make-up, painted to enhance the windows of the soul, are all carefully articulated. She dresses in layers of silky orange hues. Fastening, tying, pinning and putting in place final touches, she layers skirt and fabric, bangles, coins and beads. She is almost ready. Stretching, reaching, and twirling with apprehensive happiness, she thinks, "Let the dance begin."

She awaits her announcement. Then, infused with music and drum beat, with veils and zills for accompaniment, she makes her entrance. Her feet hold fast to the ground, rooted in contact with earth. Footsteps touch, glide and hold, never leaping or soaring, that would leave the earth bereft, and so she stays intimate. Hip rhythms increase as the drums strengthen. Shakes and shimmies move with intelligent accent. Intention weaves through her pelvis with a celestial pulse. Sound waves merge with cells that gyrate in precise rhythm. It is not only her expertise. It is cosmic harmony. It is happening now, in this moment. All her sensations happen in the now. Dance happens in the now.

Ecstatic sparks move to the heart in celebratory joy. They fly toward the heavens. And so her arms reach up and undulate grace. Her hands open and close, caressing the air like sea anemones swaying in ocean current. Her supple fingers grasp at nothing, as if trying to catch angel feathers too ethereal to hold. Fields of flowers extending toward sunlight as soft winds ripple through them, move like her body moves. She is all the elements: earth, air, fire, water, and ether, shaking, quivering, and spiraling upward. Her mind is now filled with beauty and the Oneness of all things. She is beautiful. She is loved. The cosmic play that whispers sensations of eternity is here. She loves to dance with eternity.

Veil of Sensation

"Come back to your body...The body is the home of the soul. Come back here."
-Kyle Gray

This second veil is all about sense-feeling. It begs immersion into the sensual. Our five senses connect us to the world of being. All living creatures on earth have their unique way of sensing and connecting. You do not see with a fish eye view, nor do you have sonar, multiple eyes, or a tongue that can smell. Yet you sense and process. You can ask what the experience means. With consciousness, you find sensation, emotion, and meaning. There is deep connective knowing underneath sensation.

Your body is an instrument of transcendence. If you stay present, if you play with energy with mindfulness, and view your body with love, you come to know it as a safe path to enlightenment. In dance you study each nuance of physical experience because it leads to guided creativity. Because dance is always in the present moment, the body offers itself to all realms, to the eternal, which exists perpetually in the present.

When the mind is fully acquainted with the body, dance morphs into a moving meditation. You are close with breath, heartbeat, movement in space, and a plethora of sensory input. Then consciousness meets you there. Precisely because you are open to receiving, it meets you there. It meets you when you are open! Receiving is no easy task. You need to feel worthy in order to receive. The word Kabbalah, the name for mystical Judaism, means to receive. When you open, you are feeling and sensing freedom, ecstasy, agony, pain, fear, love, and whatever is.

Belly dancing celebrates this submersion into sensual experience. An aliveness rearranges your body chemistry, your thought-connections, and your self-view. This learning is nonverbal, even preverbal. You have synthesized experience prior to your ability to speak and hear language. This experience changes your vibration, rewires your brain, recalibrates your cells, and shakes your soul. That is why insights arise. You are more alive to what is! Dance is not simply the execution of steps. It is inherent body-knowledge of feelings that reveals truth.

Rejection of the Body

In our culture, logic is praised more than feeling. Many people shut off at the neck. You have been taught to trust reasoning more than emotion. There has been too much talk about sinfulness of body. Esoteric discourses suggest the body is corrupt. Some spiritual practices have involved denial, alienation, abuse, and avoidance of the body. Think of ascetics in the desert avoiding food, cleanliness, and even water. Chastity belts, insisting on virgin marriages, or virgin sacrifices, and taboos on pleasure have prevailed for centuries in differing forms. Pornography also contributes to a view of the body as tainted. Some forms of body hatred are just an unfortunate background hum, and other forms of body alienation cause unbearable suffering.

Her
Cut off your clitoris
Bind your feet
Take away any opinions
And trade yourself for cattle

Give away your first born daughter
Offer sex for survival
And whisper the name of the divine
As an abomination

Cut off your left side, the feminine side,
And view things with one eye
Call God only a He
And believe in the punitive

Stuff your beautiful belly into tight breathless ties
And walk on pinched toes
Cover your face
And don't vote
..........**Or**...........

Whisper the word Goddess
In your granddaughter's ear
Dance with beads and coins on your hips
And symbols on your fingers

Proclaim a beauty that shines even in old age
Speak your truth
With kindness
And breastfeed your children

Birth your boys and girls in love
And be the love you wish to receive
Share your wild woman wisdom
With a passion for the natural

Sing with the wind in your hair
And wear it any way you like
Let your anger melt like ice in the sun
Caress Mother Earth, our mother
Your mother, and your father

The feminine way of forgiveness does *not* cut anything off
We are all encompassing
Embrace all of life and
Again whisper the name of the Divine
for all to hear...as Love

-MZN

The Goddess Within

In dialogue with Bill Moyers on *The Goddess,* Joseph Campbell suggests that there exists a split in our culture between spirit and nature. Nature, seen as the female, Mother-Earth for example, has not been perceived to be as holy or powerful as the masculine-god of the heavens. Exploitation of the earth and its resources reflects disdain for the body, especially the female body. You have been taught to see natural aspects of yourself with disapproval. It has been called your "animal nature," as if animals were totally apart from us. In a heady world, feelings are relegated pejoratively to animal instincts rather than a path to mystic insight. Yet there is a need to understand this animal-self in order to know your higher-self. To understand the gifts of sensation, you must first embrace the animal intelligence in your body. Being human, you have a self awareness that can even talk about itself; animals don't do that. They have another way of knowing. Sometimes it appears that the price for this speech making is a distancing from your own body. How will you use this self-awareness? How will you use the experiential knowledge of sensing?

Do Animals Dance?

"The Owl and the Pussycat went to sea
In a beautiful pea-green boat:
They took some honey, and plenty of money
Wrapped up in a five-pound note. . .

26

They dined on mince and slices of quince,
Which they ate with a runcible spoon;
And hand in hand, on the edge of the sand,
They danced by the light of the moon,
The moon,
The moon,
They danced by the light of the moon."
—by Edward Lear

I have never walked into my living room to find my cat belly dancing! Do animals dance? They do posture, move in wild gestures, and have "dances" or ritualized moves. This is done mostly by birds, who, if truly descended from dinosaurs, have had millions of years to perfect it. I'm sure play, swimming, running and strutting could all constitute dancing, yet humans indulge in dance in a very unique way. You are able to play with your dance. You can program, learn, and engage in the act of creation, because you are human. This happens as you open fully to the present moment, with all of your senses.

"Why don't animals dance?" I asked my young granddaughter. I am fond of asking her questions. Quinn said, "Because they don't know how." "Hum," I muttered, "Then why do you dance?" And she replied "Let me dance a minute and then I'll tell you." Finally, she said "Because you feel things when you dance."

Here is what Sharon, the beautiful dancer *Seraphina* feels when she dances.

Seraphina by Sharon Chinitz

My dance name is Seraphina, the "feminine form of the Latin name *Seraphinus*. It is derived from the Biblical word *seraphim*, which in Hebrew means *fiery ones*. When I dance, I am the fiery one: warm and soothing with a white-hot passionate soul. With every spin I am infused with new breath and new possibility. Belly dance has changed my life. It has given me inner peace and a gutsy confidence I didn't know I had.

Dance is a vehicle that forces introspection, to look deeply at all aspects of our authentic selves - especially the parts we don't share with others. It is a unique and special gift, one that I have given to myself and one I can now give to others. When I dance, I connect with the earth and my earthly sisters: those here now and those who came before. We connect with all souls who accept our gift. Dance has given me friends and community, and it is a healing gift I also give back by fundraising for worthy causes. Yet, I did not seek belly dance as a form of healing. It's exotic beauty called to me, but I never sought it for therapeutic release. It all started with a mundane ad in the paper...to watch a show at a restaurant, along with a coupon to try a free class. I was 47 years old with no formal dance training.

When I dance, I am the goddess. But strangely, I am also the child. In order to dance freely, it is important to embody both. I have learned to be strong through much suffering in life. Anyone who meets me would not say that I am shy and vulnerable. Yet underneath, there still exists a small, ungraceful child seeking acceptance.

Courage and strength exhibited in belly dance has come through suffering as well. It is not all fun and shimmies. I will never forget my first classes and performances. They generated so much excitement, connection and the thrill of acceptance. However, along with smiles and applause, there also came intimidation, jealousy, shame, cattiness and pain. Women can inflict such pain on their fellow women. It is important not to let this get in the way of your journey. True friends will emerge and support you, not judge you. We grow individually but remain as one heart.

My first solo performance broke further chains. I went out and gave it my all. My fear became my fuel, and courage followed. When I dance now, I am less afraid, not just because I am a more experienced dancer, but because I have learned that it is OK to just be myself. We must be courageous enough to love ourselves and to share the gifts we have to offer. If you are hurting, show your pain. If you are happy, rejoice. Just be real.

Being a well-rounded dancer not only refers to being trained in several genres. It also refers to being in touch with your emotions.

People don't realize the huge emotional component that is present in performance. I have done extensive work over the past twenty years, with the wonderful author of this book, who helped me get in touch with my feelings enough to dance them freely. During a painful time in my life, I had joined a gym because I was not proud of my body. That is where I met her. She was the first person who told me that I had a beautiful body...and she made me believe it! She has been my teacher and friend ever since.

I currently take private lessons with Samira, another teacher who supports me with her whole heart. She is the real deal and graciously shares her time, knowledge and love of dance. She is tough and challenges me. I love and respect her. Now, I am proud of the belly and hips that brought me two children...hips that can also shake the earth.

Through the course of my journey I have been invited to perform. There are many younger, more advanced dancers in the performance world. I think "Why on earth would people want me?" Then I realize, I have something to offer, and I am being invited! Someone liked my performance and requested that I go on a stage with these very accomplished dancers. When I am envious of the beautiful, thin, young dancers with perfect technique, I re-focus my envy into acceptance. Ultimately, I know that every dancer is unique.

I've adopted a *what do I have to lose* attitude. Whatever I lack in technique I make up for in personality and authentic connection. To be a beautiful dancer one must surrender. Being a dancer is not just a progression of skills or perfect technique. It is a roller coaster of emotional growth. When you grow as a dancer, you grow as a human being. Every step is a learning experience. The one who is vulnerable and raw, courageous and willing to bare not only body, but soul, is the true dancer. She can dance until she cries, or spin into ecstasy as she opens to complete joy. She gives and she takes.

Dance is the ultimate catharsis. Close to the end game, a dancer must surrender to whatever comes her way. She must persevere. This is my current obsession...with the solitary goal of only being better than myself.

Body Play

As with Sharon, you can learn from dance expression. Open your arms and look to the sky. What do you feel? Cross your arms over your chest and look down, what do you feel now? Did you learn early-on how to experience these expressions, or were you born knowing?

When you learn to dance, you learn feeling. There is a give and take, an exchange of energy between moving and innate knowing. This exchange is a feedback loop. You feel, so you make a move, or you make a move, so you feel.

In meditation, the first awareness addresses bodily sensation, then the mind, then emotion, and finally bliss. After dense vibrations of matter are satisfied, you come into spirit. Belly dancing personifies this process. It makes you feel more than think. Even if you are following choreography, after a time, thoughts drop away and the body goes on automatic pilot...just to let you feel. You discover self expression, and in turn, that expression teaches you about yourself.

An open armed gesture exposes the heart. A figure eight hip circle awakens your sexual awareness. Belly dance erases inhibition and welcomes your exotic self. Internal calibrations reveal body as a dense expression of Divine emanation, not just a physical machine.

It is the feeling of flying that most dancers crave. The body is carried to flow state. You practice discipline of mind and body for this forthcoming freedom. You fine tune your instrument for this place of abandon. You surrender to the muse of art so you can merge with more than your personal limited existence. This is why artists, and you are an artist, understand a wide perception of reality. It becomes transpersonal. Your body already knows this union of bliss and ecstasy. It wants to tell you about it!

Jeanette by Jeanette Geraci

Inspiration is defined as "a divine influence or action on a person believed to qualify him or her to receive and communicate sacred revelation." When inspiration drives me to move to music, my conscious mind yields to impulse. My thoughts come to rest. I soften into my physical body, becoming pure instinct: self-trusting, hyper-aware, and absolutely present. My body transforms into a vehicle for intuitive expression that unlocks me and enables me to convey what I could never convey in words. Belly dance, specifically, beckons to me, begging me to speak in its ancient language of shimmies and undulations. My spirit dances and my flesh follows suit, rippling in its radiant and abundant feminine lushness. I am ripening, flowering, overflowing. My entire body takes on the quality of water; the element that sustains life. If only for an instant, my ego dissolves and something else compels me to move. That something else is me...bare, distilled, and unapologetic. My cells perceive and communicate truth. When I dance, I return to my animal self. How fervently the life force snakes through me, shoots to and out of every limb and follicle. Each atom of my body is electric, kinetic, turned on. When I surrender myself to that powerful energy source deep within, I feel God drawing air into my lungs. In turn, I breathe out my dance.

Control and Freedom

As a woman, you can get swept up in emotional currents. Especially when the collective experiences of puberty, sexual awakening, pregnancy, and menopause lead you to question what is happening. Belly dancing encourages you not to reject your body, and its many stages of metamorphosis, but instead to see each change as a great gift. The feminine body experience can carry you into wise knowing.

Interestingly, belly dance also contains the restrained moves of one who is not free, like the hip-hop step *running man*, which stays in place while running. What would it feel like to run from the ghetto, or poverty, or to dance free of the harem, in an oppressive society? Would it be a dance of oppression or expression; or perhaps both? Belly dance snakes in waves of involutionary energy. Wild gyrations vibrate without going anywhere. They turn back into the self.

Belly dance has at times a quality of controlled power with nowhere to go. Then the paradox begins. The inward moves create a sense of freedom. The undulations remind us of new life. Rocking-swaying hips make you feel as if you are traveling, even while standing still. Emotions leap from your heart to become a smile. Belly rolls and belly flutters celebrate voluptuous roundness. You find that you are a woman doing a women's dance: a Goddess belly dancing. And somehow you feel free.

Yet, sometimes the orange veil attracts too much attention. You become fixated, frustrated, and unable to look away from its attractive light. You get caught-up in too much freedom, too much sensuality. It may cause a hijacking of your self-control. Too much of a good thing is not good. With freedom comes responsibility. If the responsibility is ignored you are out of balance. This is what happened to me as I opened to the orange veil of sensation. But first, let's look at the seven wisdoms and see what they offer as a peek behind the orange veil:

Seven Wisdoms

As you will see, all Seven principles imply sensing and feeling at this level. Here is how the other seven insights and traditions name this sensual time.

- In *Deepak Chopra's Seven Spiritual Laws of Success* he lists:

   Give and Receive

   This giving and receiving is the flow of sensation. It is the dancer and the audience, the moves and the feelings, the flow of your breath into the air and back to your lungs. It is the giving of gratitude for your dance, and the grace you receive back. It is ecstatic energy and rest. Belly dance embodies giving and receiving. The orange veil embodies giving and receiving.

- *In The Yogi's Seven Stages of Development before Achieving Complete Liberation*, it is stated:

   The Yogi recognizes the causes of his sufferings,
   uses this knowledge to free himself from these
   causes and hence becomes free from pain.

The Yogi is aware of sensations and the meanings of sensation. As stated, this understanding to free oneself of suffering uses the knowledge of sensation. This comes through intimate acquaintance with sensation, the same thing required in dance. You feel the body in order to transcend it. You go into it to come out.

• In the *Seven chakras the Second Chakra is:*

> *Svadisthana, the self-sustaining sacral*
> *chakra, just above the pubic bone.*

This chakra is associated with the water element. Feelings flow like water. The color oranges signifies this chakra. It is centered around feelings, and the right to feel. Connected to our sensing abilities and life's sensual pleasures, creativity and the ability to play, it is also related to social and intimacy issues. This chakra governs reproduction, vitality, creativity, joy, spirituality, and enthusiasm. All these descriptions align with the orange veil: self sustenance into creation, feeling into meaning, and sensuality into creativity. Also sex leading to birth, as an example of creativity.

• *In Lawrence Kohlberg's Stages of Moral Development, Stage 2 is:*

Naively egoistic orientation...Right action is that which is instrumental in satisfying the self's needs and occasionally others'. Relativism of values to each actor's needs and perspectives. Naive egalitarianism, orientation to exchange and reciprocity.

You can see that this again coincides with giving and receiving, self sustaining, and satisfying the self, which may bring to mind sensuality, and the sense of satisfaction. It also reflects the idea that this immersion into the sensual can at times cloud higher judgment.

- Dr. Clarissa Pinkola Estes discusses the second stage of love as such:

> *The chase and the hiding...a time*
> *of hopes and fears for both.*

Trying to outrun the mysterious "life, death, life cycle," is what she refers to as the major challenge of love. It causes lovers to play hide and seek with their feelings of fear and love. These fears are exhibited through chasing and hiding from one another. While they try to avoid being with the challenges of relationship, they finally learn to accept their feelings.

- In *Buddhism's Seven Factors of Enlightenment*, the second stage is:

> *Investigation, damma vicaya, of dhammas.*

In Buddhism, Dharma means "cosmic law and order," but it is also the term for "phenomena." Phenomena, is any observable occurrence. Phenomena are often, but not always, understood as "appearances" or "experiences." So the investigation of what is going on is then seen, felt, heard, or known through deepening into the senses.

- ***The Second Mystical Secret: The Orange Veil of Sensation: Sensation Unveils Insight***

> *"Flashes of intuition will come and go, and you*
> *will discover a secret here...you will understand*
> *the mystery of God on your own."*
> -Daniel C. Matt, from *The Essential Kabbalah*

As you experience sensation, exquisite insights will be gifted to you. This is the second stage of healing the soul. Encountering phenomenon, without denial, allows you to really feel. You acquire a taste for feeling, like acquiring a taste for fine wine, or cheese, or anything that might seem strange at first. That opening, that awareness to being fully present, is what unwraps insight, the gifted knowing. It is not logical.

This gift takes you further along the path toward enlightenment. A broad range of sense-shifting and shape-shifting is met. You feel comfortable and uncomfortable. A spectrum of sensate knowing widens. This orange veil exemplifies "*felt-sense.*" It reflects the first time you get a sense that something is not-quite-right. It is a welcoming of "gut level" feelings: that sharp or hazy sense of significance. It welcomes intuition. What you feel has value, even grand intelligence. Not allowing for this "*felt-sense*" disembodies knowledge. You were given a body for a reason. You were given feelings for a reason. "E-motion" reminds you that feelings move through you. They change and morph your psyche and chemistry. Being with them leads to breakthrough insightfulness.

Experiential Dance Activities*:*

- ○ *Talk-Dance*: As you belly dance accentuate parts of your body by moving your hands gracefully above them, and say "These are my life giving breasts, this is my life giving belly, these are my hips...I am rocking the cradle of civilization." Learn to feel and acknowledge your body as you move.
- ○ *Hip Sway:* sway your hips like a cradle, dance-rocking a baby in your arms, then in your hips. Use your collective consciousness where secrets are stored, and try feeling on for size. See what you *know* about being a mother rocking her baby.
- ○ *One Step:* Do one belly dance step, for example the cha-cha, with different feelings: angry, happy, sad, nervous, sexy, and more. Experience how different motions become different e-motions, as the dance transforms into slightly differing expressions.
- ○ *Dance a Mythological Character* or fairy tale character to see how it feels to be her. Sink into the character-acting feeling with your whole body. For example, be Cinderella.

- ○ *Fast Song Change*: Play music, and have someone change the song every few seconds. Dance to any song before it changes quickly to another. See and feel how the music changes you.
- ○ *Change directions* deliberately as you dance: up, down, forward, and back, acknowledge how a change in direction changes your perspective.

My Story in The Orange Veil

"To me the body says what words cannot."- Martha Graham

During certain decades of my youth, sexual mores were being questioned. The birth control pill, women's rights, hippie lifestyles, free-love, peace and love, and playing with anti-establishment ways were all up for exploration. My first husband, brilliant, and sensitive to the changing times, while attending Harvard, began to have reservations about traditional marriage. He had been studying moral development, and was perhaps questioning his own beliefs. That's when I was first introduced to studies on moral development; the human development department at Harvard was our academic social circle.

After discussion on the subject for years, we still debated passionately. It was a painful time for both of us. I thought I wanted exclusive intimacy. Of course, I know that marital challenges don't form in a vacuum. We each had our own woundedness to contend with, as everyone does, and how to address it was not clear at that time. I had not yet learned the full measure of compassion or forgiveness as healing elixirs. At this time, we had two small children. He shared his ideology, and I had choices. Get a divorce, do nothing, or have an open marriage: when spouses openly agree to be with other people. There are presumably no concealed arrangements, but tell that to a heart!

Subliminally, my first intention when learning belly dance was to become the sexiest woman alive. I was going to be desired and loved! The only trouble is, it doesn't work that way. One does not find love through righteous anger or self destructive ways of being. The not-so-pretty knowing of sensuality feels it all. After denial under the red veil,

36

came the orange veil of heightened senses. My innocence was now gone, so my senses became very keen for survival.

"Heightened Senses"

My desire to feel became stronger than my need to be blind. I was an awakened animal with better hearing, smelling, and yearning impulses. Libidinal energy was flowing through my veins. I wanted to be loved...physically. I used my beauty, strength, and grace to be adored. I craved strong arms, adoring eyes, and masculine strength to enter me and reaffirm my essence. I was performing for love, yet not truly receiving it.

I've been in love many times in my life, but not really. Egoic love is never restful. The quest was actually for self love, and at the time I couldn't find it in another. Each man that loved me offered different gifts. One read me poetry, one wrote me poetry, another had exquisite caress, and another heroic gestures. Even marriage was offered, but I was not free. Not within myself. My sensuality was on fire but I could not truly believe. That came later.

Feeling beyond sensation means finding meaning, and so my feelings had to go deeper. Feelings fluctuate, meaning holds sway for a while, but only insight brings clarity. Even now I count on sensations to reveal higher truth...not logic alone.

This love-making, dancing time, was my kinesthetic response to loneliness and God-longing. And so it came. Secretly, this was the beginning of seeking knowledge of the self, and of the Divine.

I came from a quite innocent, protected background, with thank God, no physical or sexual abuse. I had a loving family where perfectionism might have been the greatest challenge. Subtle criticism threatened my self esteem, but nothing prepared me for the devastation I experienced in marriage. After the crying and the rage, a determination to find my sexual self rose up like a striking cobra. I wanted to be loved for that. After all, sex was the insult, so it had to be the answer.

"Open" sounded free and easy, didn't it? Or, was it the cutting edge, avant-garde attitude of rebellion, that attracted me? My confusion fueled my avoidance. It helped me avoid deeper knowing. We were pushing the envelope of ordinary restricted life. We were cool and compromising, or so it seemed in my state of denial. But when I found myself feeling unbearably rejected, it seemed to threaten my very sense of self. I was sad, extremely sad, and very angry at not being loved. But I was feeling! I hired a babysitter, while I was at home, so I could cry and contemplate life and death. After crying for hours, a still small voice reminded me that *I* loved myself. It seemed to say *I love you*. It came from somewhere deep within my heart, like a tiny spark. As I was crying, and clinging to a large towel, this inner-knowing called to me. Like the swans overhead, or the smiling faces of my mother and father, or the love of my body, or the needs of my adorable children with their gracious love...something was calling...something small but true. I did love myself. I heard it. I felt it. It was true. This was my beginning of insight.

This was my first "dark night of the soul." After being tangled in the red veil that told me I couldn't survive, that I had to pretend, that I could only play at love, because it might not be real, I was finally able to unwrap. I could feel the orange veil. I felt euphoric highs as well as pain and suffering. It allowed me to wallow in self pity for a time, to cry, sob, shake, and cry again until my energy seemed to all but fade away.

That tiny inner voice was a light on the path. It was the beginning of my path to God: the unnamable all-knowing One. It was not actually a voice. It was silent. It came as an insight from my soul—and beyond, communicating with me. This way of understanding lead me much further at a later time, a time of complete dimensional shift. I will tell you about it in a forthcoming veil.

The dance wove in and out of the tapestry of my experience. It was where I felt my feelings, expressed my longings, shared my gifts, and ultimately found who I really was.

The lessons of this painful time, even when my heart was closed to truth, lead to the groundbreaking changes needed for my soulful quest. Joan Borysenko says:

> *"The times when we are most aware of the heart opening*
> *is when it has been closed."*

It is inevitable to explore the darkness beyond denial into sensing. As you flow with the tides of your dilemmas, the storms subside, and you learn to ride the waves of life and death. Facing and feeling the darkness helps you see the light.

Sensing Love and Fear

It's been said that there are only two emotions: love and fear. You are not a sharp toothed mammal with claws. You don't have bristly fur for protection. You do have a sharp mind acutely aware of danger. This is your biological system of protection. Stress hormones like norepinephrine and cortisol flood the body, and adrenaline is released during stress. Part of spiritual development is to be with your stress and fear. It asks you to explore how you will provide for yourself and others. It guides you away from danger toward safety. As long as you do not label or define yourself as fearful, oversensitive, or not brave, you can let the emotion move through you and learn from it.

Similarly, love is a strong emotion. When you fall in love, which has been said to take a fifth of a second, according to research, your body chemistry changes. It is as if a veritable pharmacy were at your disposal. You get a euphoric high of dopamine, adrenaline, oxytocin and norepinephrine. Some are similar to the hormones released during fear. You may blush, have sweaty palms and a racing heart…and furthermore, you like it!

It's been noted that kissing gives a women a dose of testosterone from her manly lover. Kissing can increase your sex drive. Besides being a mood elevator, hormones actually help you bond better. Love increases your lifespan too. It has been said that being in love reduces the risk of cancer, high blood pressure, strokes, and depression. By having sex once a week you can build immunity, and reduce the risk of getting a cold. You even sleep better after having sex.

Some of these same feelings arise when you fall in love with belly dancing. No, there has probably never been a formal study on this subject from any notable university, yet I would venture to guess that the high you get from performing is a lot like being in love. You adore how enticement plays with your emotions as you dance.

In life, we all experience love and fear. Most of the time if you act out of fear there are more negative consequences than when you act out of love. Love is kind, fear is not.

So what happens when fear prevents you from acting altogether?

Stage Fright

> *"One of the deepest longings of the human soul*
> *is to be seen."*— John O'Donohue

When you are learning to dance, especially to perform, you are asked to overcome the fear of stage fright. You may be afraid of being judged, or failing, or being exposed. A myriad of other obsessions with the self come up. To overcome stage fright you take the risk of being seen. Being seen is actually something you secretly long for. Many of my mind-body clients and dance students say that they felt invisible as children. Their ideas and feelings were not acknowledged.

Overcoming stage fright, or performance anxiety, exposes the knowledge that you have something unique to offer. That uniqueness *is* you. No one else can offer it. If you keep the dance to yourself, it will never be seen. If you express it, you can give and receive love.

This brings to mind an important performance for me. I was to do *The Dance of the Seven Veils!* These veils have been with me for some time! My grandmother used to talk about that dance when I was little. It sounded so mysterious. I felt close to her as I decided to perform this dance. Using seven veils takes practice, creativity, and co-ordination. I had my plan and was carefully rehearsed. But the situation was frightening for another reason. I was new to performing. And this show had a large audience studded with well-known dancers and their families. Thinking of this discerning audience made me even more nervous. It was an important debut.

Soon everything was ready. I was about to go on. I was announced. As I entered the large stage, erected just for this event, there was an unevenness in the floor boards. One plank was definitely irregular. I did a hopping leaping trip. It was not at all appropriate for this earthy dance. I didn't exactly fall on my face, but I did falter in an ungainly way. Then a strange thing happened. I felt as if any possible mistake was now over, and it seemed funny. The silly faltering almost caused me to laugh out loud, so I smiled...a really big smile...and suddenly I became free.

What I remember most now, is the aftermath of that successful performance. I sat alone backstage, slumped in a chair, holding all the crumpled seven veils, while trying to catch my breath. My heart was still dancing. My breath heaved. I felt as if I had been running a high speed race. Then a huge pleasurable feeling of openness and gratitude came to me. I was so happy it broke my heart open. I had "danced my heart out" and it was fabulous! I loved myself. I loved everything in that joyous moment.

In the following story, the beautiful dancer Rebecca describes her "stage fright" before trying to belly dance. This was her time in the orange veil.

Rebecca's Story by Rebecca Ness

Elvis, male belly dancers, seventies inspired parties, limos to "The Belly Dance Superstars!" Who wouldn't want some lovin' from The King, or to wear a long black wig, big sunglasses, shiny bell bottoms and look like Cher? These were some of the many themed parties that had been revealed to me by my good friend and yoga teacher, Davira. This was some juicy stuff, but how do I get into the "club?"

There is some debate as to who pushed me over the edge. Was it my homeopath, Francine? She had given me some pellets and told me I'd wake up one morning feeling all feminine and in touch with my G-d given, girly talents. Or was it Davira who continued to entice me with little tidbits of info about her belly dance friends? There was a core group of women that had been coming for years. The group consisted of a thrift shop belly queen, a sassy and sexy psychologist, a mother of five with a wicked sense of humor, a Russian optometrist, just to describe a few. The women were all different shapes, sizes, and ages. I had my own story to tell but would I fit in?

> *"Locked in this dance is a secret language that*
> *tells the story of women's lives.*
> *Their passions and their spirituality, their*
> *sacrifices, their joys. Their intuitions,*
> *their emotional dreams"...Delilah*

As I was told I would, I took the plunge. I dove in, with little courage and a whole lot of trepidation. Starting something new always scared me. For years I had suffered from severe panic attacks caused by social phobia. Hives, rapid heartbeat, y'know, where the blub-dub sound is so loud you can hear it thrashing against your eardrums? Included in these attacks were the shakes and beads of sweat secreting from every pore in my body...the whole nine yards. I would have attacks in the most interesting places. One time I passed out at my in-laws thanksgiving table. I was married just 2 months, and mortified that they would think I had passed out because I was pregnant...which I was not! Another time, I was in a bio-chemistry class in college, standing at the professor's desk, about to ask him a question, and boom, I blacked out and hit the floor like a ton of bricks.

A respected hospital in my area was doing a study on panic attacks. I threw myself into that study so fast, I even shocked myself. With intense therapy, eventually I overcame most of my social anxiety. Much of it involved feeling the fear, exploring the worst that could happen, and "doing it anyway." When physical sensations became uncomfortable, almost unbearable, I was motivated to genuinely feel and accept my deepest feelings. I disliked being so constricted when I couldn't allow my views or mindset to be expressed! I was afraid that expressing my feelings would cause me to be judged and rejected. This does rear its ugly head every so often, but not to the extreme, thank G-d. It is only a subtle reminder that life is too short to deny myself expression. The remnants reminded me to live every waking moment with awareness, love and harmony. There is no time or place for staying stuck in fear. Now I know that it is ok to feel fear, and to accept that it is part of my personal growth.

So here I was, confronting my fear. Would I be good at belly dancing? I had taken ballet for many years as a child and young adult, but belly dance seemed so much more…sensual. Would I embarrass myself? Would I have a debilitating panic attack?

A big part of what got me in the door was the idea of the underground sisterhood. The shows, the laughs, and the camaraderie they had with one another really interested me. It seemed kind of secretive too, and that was exciting. I wanted to be a part of something unique and different and, by George, I was going to do it. I faced the fear, I screwed the fear, and off I went! There was too much that I wanted that overpowered the fear. To my relief, I was welcomed with open arms, which completely reassured and encouraged me. Who cares anyway if you look like a camel with three humps?

"Hold your hands out gently; ask others to do the same. See how different each person looks. Each person has their own unique and natural beauty. Use this natural beauty when you dance. Respect your individuality."…Artemis

For some reason it had not occurred to me that the art of belly dance was to be aware of the belly. I did not take into account that I was required to look at my body in the mirror, and wholly accept the area between my neck and thighs. Now here's the thing, my belly is graced with battle scars as a result of a twin pregnancy, and a single one soon after. I despised my stomach. I hated it with a passion. Sometimes I would yell at it, fight with it, and tell it to go back to its original position.

At this moment, as I expose my innermost fears, I realize that growing up with a family member who had an eating disorder did in fact have an effect on me. I thought she was a perfect 10. I wanted to look like her, dress like her, be her. But I knew I could never harm my body the way she harmed hers. So I finally put my focus on something that made me feel strong and courageous...karate. I persevered and became a black belt and a fierce competitor. I traveled around the USA as well as Israel, and won numerous medals and trophies...some were even bigger than me! I was in the best shape of my life. I continued off and on for years after my children were born. But there was a certain strangeness about stepping into a shapeless and colorless gi (the belt had my name stitched in gold Japanese letters, but that doesn't count). Later I would run over to belly dance class and slip on a number that made me feel somewhat feminine. So here I was kicking some ass at 9 and attempting a shimmy at 11. Undulations were hard enough for me to learn, did I really need to make them harder by getting the occasional blow to the solar plexus?

"Dance is work, hard work, and not just physical, but emotional and intellectual and spiritual. You gotta be fearless, or at least unafraid to face your fears and ride through it coming out stronger. Challenge yourself to push for the best, not just diddle around. Take it seriously, love it, hate it, fight it, dance with it. Jump off the dang cliff and go for it!"...Baraka

As time went by, I decided to quit karate and give my dance the undivided attention it deserved. I added more flare to my outfits, applied cat eyes, and interestingly became attracted to all things shimmery, shiny, or glittery. I can even tolerate, dare I say, leopard! With all the love I was giving to my body, making it even more beautiful, it was hard to ignore the hidden love I knew I had for that one body part. Housing and nourishing my babies for 18 months total was no small feat. As the appreciation grew, the scars seemed to fade in my mind's eye. I had a new confidence in and out of class that started to blossom. I was now feeling like the free, fearless woman I was born to be.

These days I laugh when I think about how easy it was to create my 6 pack abs during my karate heydays. They prepared me for the "sexy ab contest" my family has on a weekly basis...I have three sons. Now I know it was also getting me ready to perform expert belly undulations, flutters, and rolls.

My fear of acceptance is practically non-existent now, as a result of the love and positive energy that endlessly flows from the sisterhood. I can do no wrong, except maybe run off to a last minute belly dance show or get a spontaneous henna tattoo and not inform everyone beforehand. I love what I am a part of. I love that they are a part of me. I love the love that is being instilled in me each and every class. I love that I am learning each and every day to just be me. I thank each and every one of my sisters, and my family. I hope that they will all be rewarded with 120 years, in return for giving me the ability to love and appreciate the physical body that vessels (harnesses) my soul...Amen.

Opening to Sensation

As you open to sensation, you begin to experience the insight of spirit. It is the expression of the body before consciousness. Although your body will leave when the time comes, in the meanwhile, it holds your soul like a mother holds her newborn. Cherish it. Know it. Listen to it.

"The philosopher's soul dwells in his head, the poet's soul is in his heart; the singer's soul lingers about his throat, but the soul of the dancer abides in all her body."— Kahil Gibran

Dance is the art of feeling in motion. You merge with energy in a momentous matching of time. Like fusion, you collide with it, and are thereby changed by it. This is healing. You might stay wrapped in the orange veil for a while, but the spiritual awakening will not be stopped. This sensing of insight will lead you to keen observation. What do you wish to see now? The next veil is calling to you. What veil is next?

CHAPTER 3

THE YELLOW VEIL

The Third Veil: The Yellow Veil of Observation

"Observation"

> *All perceiving is also thinking, all reasoning also intuition, all observation also invention.* - Rudolf Arnheim, art and film theorist, and gestalt psychologist

Do you see it? Everywhere you look inviting yellow light is shining. It holds great energy. You are dancing with the yellow veil. It brings warmth and vibrancy. It seems to have fiery golden mirrors fastened within its folds.

Yellow is the most luminous color of the visible spectrum. Gleaming, blond, silky hair, sunflowers, daffodils, egg yolks, ripe lemons, and bumble bee stripes all suggest optimism. And sometimes caution. It is here, enveloped by the yellow veil, that your sensual awareness begins to highlight a burning curiosity. Brightness offers perspective. You see showers of light before the veil appears. Then as the veil swirls away, you see a lingering aftermath. You intuit ethereal awareness. Brilliance is always transforming. As you dance with this veil your eyes shine with delight. The yellow veil reveals who you are, and who you are becoming. It also reflects the changing world around you. Your attentiveness illuminates this inner and outer expose'.

All this seeing ignites a "fire in the belly." The upper belly above your naval is where the fire glows. You see the light of this glow. Like watching fireplace flames, you become fascinated. Follow the light. Can you direct it? What is it showing you? What is this "fire in the belly" illuminating for you?

Veil of Observation

"The very existence of the seen is for the sake of the seer." -Patanjali

Once you wiggle out of the red veil of denial and remove the orange veil of sensation, you are enveloped by the yellow veil of observation. Here you begin to see yourself. You may think: "Is that me? Do I look like that? Am I changing?"

Consider the eerie sensation of being watched by a portrait painting. One that maintains eye contact from every vantage point. Your own eyes are watching you like that. They see and mirror your egoic-self as well as your higher-self. This portraying is sometimes favorable, sometimes not. As you look through eyes of kindness, you will learn to see more clearly. Then you can use your entire being to observe.

Reflections are everywhere in your environment: the people, your experiences, and your thoughts and feelings. You are the silent witness, the observer, the one who is watching. It is not a visual watching. It is internal. This embodiment is intelligent. It is the awareness of the nature of your consciousness. It is the awareness of awareness. It is the beginning of becoming awake to your creations, especially the creation of your "self." In belly dance, these watched emotions morph into choreography, story, symbol, and art. You can see yourself in the art, and as the art!

Sunrise Dance

Watching the sunrise, you hear a bird symphony. The wind rushes through trees whispering and roaring. The distant ocean adds its clash of sound. There are no cell phones, televisions, or computers. There is only landscape and sound. What do you do for entertainment? You talk, tell stories, draw, and you dance. This is not for amusement. It is for communion with the natural.

Your dance is imaginative and serious. It conveys cultural values. It reveals desire and hope. It coaxes Divine intelligence to watch over you. You beg it to heal your tribal members. It evokes your ancestors in a cry for help, and for the passing of knowledge. It brings body-memory to the fore. You count on it for endurance, as you act and reenact dances that emulate challenges. You conjure spirits both sacred and scary. You call forth forces of good for protection. The dance is magical. It is your link to spirit world. You dance to procreate; to create. It is a solemn act summoning the law of attraction. Like a child in deep play, you are lost in drums, windful flutes, chants, and song. You share tribal mystical ecstasy to ensure life. You observe everything, with every part of your being. You dance to create connection of heaven to earth, and you belong to both realms. You dance to the all-knowing intelligence and love that runs everything.

DNA maps the moves. Like $E=MC^2$, rhythm becomes a metaphor for energy. Energy changes into matter...at the speed of dance. The dance charts the harmony of galaxies with your heartbeat. The light of which you are made wants to move with you because it must. You play with it. You play to create. Your entire observing is engrossed in a dance with the cosmos.

In the yellow veil, you emerge with a new world view. In order to see this view, you must transform the way you see.

My Story in The Yellow Veil

What I've learned through belly dance helped me recover from a very trying time in my life. It lead me into self-realization. This will be explored in further veils. It helped me heal. But first I had to *see* what was going on.

At the height of my professional dance career, I was injured in a car accident. I remember asking the driver to slow down. The slow motion view of being driven into a telephone pole is forever etched in my psyche. Moments later, writhing in pain on the ground, I became aware of scorching fiery sensations around my back and abdomen. My nervous system was on fire. I was unable to move. My back was broken.

People covered me with coats as they stood vigil; while from some inexplicable distance, I heard myself moaning. My brother Russell, also a passenger, stayed with me until the ambulance arrived. His soothing words gave me courage. It was only after the EMT's arrived that he revealed his own dislocated shoulder and broken collar bone. We ended up sharing the ambulance. As I write this, I am reminded of his heroic nature. He went on to become a doctor who specialized in emergency surgery, and also a Colonel in the Army. He has offered this same kind of help to many others during the war in Iraq, as well as in his daily life at home. He is brave and compassionate.

As a result of this accident, my dance career froze to an abrupt halt. So did many things in my life. My father was dying of stomach cancer just as my mother was diagnosed with breast cancer, and my divorce was waiting in the wings. While all this was happening, I was in a steel back brace. I was not capable of moving, let alone dancing. Frustration and deep sorrow arose and fell with ferocious tenacity. It was an astonishing time of extreme physical and emotional pain. Along with the inability to move, I was in fact, trapped in my life— not just my body. It was time to stop and observe. I needed clarity. I needed to see my own behavior. I needed to see all the ways I was not being true to my precious existence.

When I was lying in the hospital bed, the doctor came to discuss my diagnosis. He told me my back was broken. I said "You mean I can't dance?" I surprised myself with this response. You'd think I would have replied, "You mean I can't take care of my children?" or "I can't have sex, or I can't walk?" Yet I said, "You mean I can't dance?"

Of all freedoms, I would miss this lifeline the most. I had been using my dance to get me through the day-to-day sorrowful feelings of being unloved. I was clinging to belly dancing. It was a fantasy place of pleasure, with basically no pain. After the accident, not being able to dance changed all that. What was to happen? Now, I could not dance away the pain. What was my sensuality teaching me now? What was to happen next? There was something I needed to "see."

During this time of recovery I observed many thoughts: "What if I am never able to dance again? Who am I if I am not a dancer? And what is going on in my life?" I felt my body. It was not a dancer's body. I felt flaccid muscles where I used to be toned and strong. I experienced feeling crippled. I pondered life perpetually lived in a wheel chair. I imagined growing old. I imagined others growing old, frail, and weak. I observed myself feeling compassion for those who could not walk, and for those who had never danced.

I noticed that when recuperating from a sick or injured condition you are brought back to a child-like state. Like infant helplessness, you lose independence, much as the aged and moribund experience. Sickness, disease, injury, and trauma bring a "little death." Unlike a slow natural passage of days, this "la petite mort," as I came to call it, is a different progression. The term "la petite mort" is usually used to describe deep sexual release. Here, I'm taking the liberty to imply that it is a part of you that has died. It represents some ending of an era in your life.

What happens after a "little death?" Eventually a poignant enchantment with life occurs. Having received a second chance, you feel gratitude.

After my "little death," a most insightful observation occurred. I learned that being cured requires more than physical healing. The art of healing necessitates emotional and spiritual work as well. And, like the art of dance, it requires knowing and observing the self.

As I progressed in strength, knowledge of my profound gift of dance became more and more of a miracle to me. I had been blessed to dance at all! Now I was being taught patience and acceptance. I learned to receive help. The ability to "observe" that I had used in dance, was now required while I was static. I learned that the body is a metaphor for consciousness. I learned that my soul needed healing as much as my body. I was dancing with the yellow veil of observation. Watching became my occupation. I needed it. I needed to use all this knowledge. This time, I needed it to heal my life.

Observation takes many forms. Lisa Michelle, my daughter, learned many things by watching. As she activated her imagination and grace, her own "dance" took form. One of the greatest gifts in the world is to have a child. It is a blessing to have a daughter. In a mother-daughter relationship, with gratitude for this cherished bond, so much beauty arises.

But what special challenges emerge if your mother is a belly dancer? What is it like growing up with a woman like that? When I asked my daughter to write a piece for my forthcoming book, this is what she wrote. She is a writer, as well as an English teacher and yoga teacher. I am honored to share this with you. Here is her story in the yellow veil.

Daughter of the Dancer

by Michelle Spokes

Our dining room had no table. It had mirrors and a wood floor. There was a flat wrought iron heating grate by the doorway to the kitchen; this square of warmth was my seat during rehearsals.

Silas, dark-skinned and kinetic, smiling and nodding, played doumbek -- all the rhythms: chifiatelli, beledi, the drum solo. Following rehearsals, he'd stay to teach my little brother to drum. Patrick, large, gap-toothed and Indian, sat cross-legged with the sitar on his lap. Around the kitchen table later, he told stories of his birth, his entrance to this world through the trunk of his mother, the elephant. Jill, an older formidable woman with her hair colored a light blond, completed the band. She stood behind the organ in her long dresses of peacock blue or pastel green or black edged with gold. Her presence made a statement, but she never said much. Sometimes, instead of Silas, Ayed drummed. Middle Eastern like the dance itself, and in the Midwest, like we all were, Ayed had a sense of style in keeping with the times. He drove a black Trans Am with a red eagle on the hood.

Late nights on the weekends, they performed at venues like the Sahara, but on weekend afternoons, I was their audience. My mother always threw her veil to me. The veil caught the air and floated, gauzy, landing with a light touch on my face.

For dancing, she called herself Kismet, meaning destiny or fate, sounding like charisma, which dances in the helixes central in her cells.

On Sunday mornings, I was audience to the grittier magic of the dance. I watched my mom tweezing shards of glass from the soles of her feet, counting wet bills onto the bedspread, and comparing a broken toe to its counterpart.

As in Hans Christian Andersen's story of the red shoes, the dance propels the dancer. Like Scheherazade, the dance leaves the story unfinished for a thousand and one nights. Both audience and dancer are entranced.

In devotion to the dance, with a deep love of every nuance, my mother never sought to possess the ephemeral. She has a gift, and so she offers this gift. To be the recipient of this beauty is among the sweetest memories of my childhood.

The earliest memory is amorphous though. At age three, the age my daughter is now, I kneeled, looking out the window while my mom practiced to a duet in a mournful language. There was such longing in the drawn-out vowels of the voices. I imagined the stories behind what they seemed like they were saying. At the same time, in the way that young children do, I connected my senses to my mother's, and I knew how she felt while she was dancing behind me. Free, even in the learning phases.

As years went on, I became myself and she became a professional dancer. She chose her name. She acquired costumes: red with clear beads, green with gold coins, a closet full of intricate bras and belts, diaphanous skirts and veils. She put on make-up. Glue-lined false eyelashes. Liquid eyeliner shaping the eyes Egyptian.

Only the eyes are glimpsed at the entrance. The veils hide the face and the body, at first. She plays the zills while she dances, the clink of finger cymbals adding accents shiny as Gustav Klimt's gold on canvas.

As she dances, the unveiling begins. The drum solo follows -- a conversation between the shimmy and the percussion, the beaded hips and the hands on the drum. It culminates in her signature move, the Turkish drop: a jump and a collapse, a landing with knees bent back beneath the skirt and the shoulders on the ground. She lands, concurrent with the last tap of the drum. Then, a silence lasting a few breaths, is visible in the movement of her ribs. The moment feels like a finale but it is a segue.

In retrospect, I see how seductive belly dancing is, and why, when I said, *My mom is a belly dancer,* everyone always asked, *A ballet dancer?* When the dancer moves along the ground, the intimacy is disarming. Divorce was chasing her marriage. She must have been proving or needing or imploring.

After the floorwork, in the sort of fascinating effect of reverse films, she rises out of a backbend, resurrecting herself, smiling to the musicians, and the audience. She loves the dance, and knows finesse. She knows how the hands direct the eye of the audience, that back in history, women danced for each other.

In origin, this dance sang a tribute to the feminine. Women taught one another the art of childbearing. As my mother says to her dance students as the roomful of them sway their hips side to side, *You are rocking the cradle of civilization.* These words elicit laughter, as they're designed to, but at the same time, they are absolutely sincere.

So, from this cradle, I was born. But I was not born to be a dancer. For all the opportunity to carry the art into the next generation, it has never spoken to me as destiny. Other callings are written, it seems. And, if I am a dancer at all, it is through a form that speaks more to those inclined to introversion: yoga practice, vinyasa. But it may be, that like color-blindness or twin children, the possibility skips a generation. My daughter, when my mother dances, doesn't drop into her imagination, or sit and watch, riveted. She dances with her grandmother. In those moments, I am content to watch them both.

Observing and Learning

It is so poignanty beautiful for me to read my daughter's perspective. Today I take her yoga classes and see how well I can keep up! You know we don't do comparisons in yoga...that was just a transient thought I had! As all parents do, I marvel at how she can now be *my* teacher. And as I observe, I watch her watching her daughter too.

Observation and Choice

> *"But if one observes, one will see that the body has its own intelligence; it requires a great deal of intelligence to observe the intelligence of the body."* —Jiddu Krishnamurti

In dance, as in yoga, visceral savvy also awakens restraint. Connecting with physical sensation is one of the best ways to have an operative control over reactivity. If you observe, embodied awareness will teach you self control.

"What is actually happening in this moment?" you may ask. The body gives your mind information on how you feel. "I am feeling hot and experiencing a fast heartbeat. I am feeling upset and angry, and sad. I can 'see' how I am feeling, and can observe what I am thinking." As you heighten awareness, you find choice. Do you react, do you express, do you remain still? Maybe you say, "I will refrain from acting out, and just feel my anger and sadness for now." Maybe you think, "I need to speak up, yet in a way that is not harmful, when I express my feeling." What do these thoughts and feeling say about who you are?

Observation brings choice. How many layers are implied by choice? Each one leads to another. Some say that every choice leads to both a positive and negative result. You are hungry. You order chicken soup... good for you, not so good for the chicken! So every step implies another alternative. Choice happens all the time in life and dance.

Art presents a wonderful practice of choice. It can be applied to create a life rich in spiritual dimension. In belly dance there is a search for cohesive construct, meaning, or at least beauty. What are your options while creating? Do you long to design? Your life is your work of art. Here is how the Seven wisdoms relate to the yellow veil of observation:

Seven Wisdoms

- *Deepak Chopra, The Seven Spiritual Laws of Success, the third law is:*

  Good actions come back.

  This "law" states that what you give out, comes back to you. Like reflections folded in the yellow veil, you see deeds and intentions reflected back to you. The yellow veil is at work mirroring and shining who you are, right back to you. Choose wisely.

- *Yogi: Seven stages of development before achieving complete liberation.* The third stage:

  "The yogi attains full discriminative knowledge of the state of samadhi, in which the Yogi is completely absorbed into The Self."

  Discrimination is key. It implies acute thinking and observation of the process as well as the doing. The Yogi/

Yogini must learn to see and make choices: choices of thought and action. When you concentrate selectively, it will lead to liberation. Who is the Self? How does observation help you find out? Who are You?

- *Yoga Chakras: the third Chakra :*

   "Manipur," the Sanskrit name for this chakra, means "full of gems." This place is at the naval and slightly above the naval. Fire element is represented here. Manipura solar plexus, naval, the place of personal power, fear, anxiety, opinion-formation, introversion, and transition from simple or base emotions to complex. Personal power: the right to think. The balance of intellect, self-confidence and ego power. Ability to have self-control and humor."

   This Chakra relates to internal observation, fire, and the color yellow. Scientists like to call the belly the second brain. It not only thinks in its own way, but also feels about what it is thinking. It joins thought and emotion in a bodily form of knowing. It observes within an integrated body that has been learning for over 200,000 years. It observes possibilities and potentialities.

- *Kohlberg's Stages of Moral Development : Stage 3:*

   Good-boy/good-girl orientation; "Orientation to approval, to pleasing and helping others. Conformity to stereotypical images of majority or natural role behavior. Action is evaluated in terms of intentions."

   This orientation predicts the seeds and concepts of further development. Precisely because the subject is trying to emulate a higher self. In order to do that, you must have some notion of what that would be. Furthermore, in acting like the "good-boy" or "good-girl" you are viewing possibilities into "becoming the one you wish to portray." Herein lies an idea of the ideal self.

- *Dr. Clarissa Pinkola Estes discusses the third stage of love as:*

  "Untangling the Skeleton: the untangling and understanding...of the life/death/life aspects of the relationship with compassion...willing to touch the non beautiful in ourselves and others...

  Living from soul versus ego: Three things differentiate living from the soul versus living from ego only. They are: the ability to sense and learn new ways, the tenacity to ride a rough road, and the patience to learn deep love over time."

In this life/death/life cycle, if you become brave enough to observe that new learning can occur, possibilities emerge. You may find forks in the road where you must choose. How you choose will likely determine who you become. Could you make choices with love?

- *Buddhism, the Seven Factors of Enlightenment, the third factor is:*

  "Energy, viriya,...also Determination." In Sanskrit; Pāli language, Viriya is a Buddhist term commonly translated as "energy, diligence, enthusiasm, or effort." It can be defined as an attitude of gladly engaging in wholesome activities, and it functions to cause one to accomplish wholesome or virtuous actions. Vīrya literally means "state of a strong man" or "manliness." In Vedic Literature, the term is often associated with heroism and virility. In Buddhism, the term more generally refers to a practitioner's "energy" or "exertion," and is repeatedly identified as a necessary prerequisite for achieving liberation.

In terms of the yellow veil, the vibrancy and energy of the luminous light which grants you the ability to see, also accesses choice of action. To choose to see with virility is heroism. If you stay in the black and white world you see only dichotomy. To observe colors and see the gradations of shades and hues, you must turn up the yellow light and see more clearly. This requires energy and determination. How do you see the experience of having a "self?"

- ***The Third Mystical Secret of the Veils: The Yellow Veil of Observation:***

Observation Unveils the Self

The yellow veil of observation reveals the self. It demonstrates how you relate to creative choice: possibilities, originality, imagination. Vision Envisions. It participates in the act of creation, the very creation of yourself. Free will is revealed. Ignorance is gone for a time. You see yourself seeing yourself.

In conscious awareness, you observe a many faceted self. Do you have a choice about how you think and feel? Do you have a choice in the making of how you are? What is your vision of the world? Do you co-create your experience?

Experiential Dance Activities:

- *Choreograph a famous story* as a group. The audience will then guess what story it is, then be the audience, and learn from looking. Trust your intuitions about meaning.
- *Belly Dance your name in space*: How does your name make you feel? What does it mean to be individually you?
- *Crayon on the floor*: You are the crayon, the floor is the paper. Dance as if you are drawing a design or picture. How do you experience your creations? Do you let them evolve until they seem to take on a "mind of their own?"

- o *Standing Dance*: Everyone sits cross-legged on the floor while the dancer stands and dances. This is a unique perspective. You look up to the dancer and see her.
- o *Photo shop*: Dance and then form a group as if posing for a photo. See the "photo" in the mirror. What do you look like to others? What is your projected group image? Does it correlate with who you think you are, and how you feel inside?
- o *Caravan image*: Dance as if you are in the desert and a caravan is approaching from the distance: You imagine seeing yourself emerging from the caravan. If you met yourself for the first time, what impression would you have of yourself? Would you like to have yourself for a friend? Who would the caravan see?
- o *Mirror Dance*: Mirror each other as you dance. Face a partner and take turns being the mirror. One leads and the other follows: Do your relationships mirror back to you the feeling that you are understood, accepted, loved?

Self- Observation, A Divine Glimpse, and a Story of Moses

In the *Journey to Self-realization* by the guru Paramahansa Yogananda, he states:

> *"It is an insult to your Self to be born, live, and die*
> *without knowing the answer to the mystery of why you*
> *were sent here as a human being in the first place.*
> *To forget God is to miss the whole point of existence. Learn to feel God."*

In the Judeo-Christian-Islamic tradition there is a story of Moses speaking to God. God speaks from a burning bush. It is part of the Exodus story in the bible. Moses at one point asks who he is, and also who God is.

Secretly brought up as an Egyptian prince, Moses is actually a descendant of Hebrew slaves. When the story commences, we see him as an infant, floating down the Nile River in a basket. His mother has placed him there for safekeeping, to save him from being killed. He is subsequently rescued by the daughter of an Egyptian pharaoh. She becomes his foster mother, and raises him as her own. Meanwhile his real mother disguises herself as a wet nurse in order to be with her son. As the story progresses you see Moses change his identity several times.

When Moses comes upon a burning bush, the voice of God speaks to him. This burning bush is on fire yet it is not consumed. The voice asks Moses to go back to Egypt to free the Hebrew slaves.

> *"Moses said to God, "Who am I that I should go to Pharaoh and bring the Israelites out of Egypt?"*
>
> *And God said, "I will be with you."*
>
> *Moses said to God, "Suppose I go to the Israelites and say to them, 'The God of your fathers has sent me to you,' and they ask me, 'What is his name?' Then what shall I tell them?"*
>
> *God said to Moses, "I AM WHO I AM. This is what you are to say to the Israelites: I AM has sent me to you."*

Literal or a parable, the story illustrates a self questioning; one that mirrors a questioning of the Divine as well. When Moses asks God, "Who am I," does he mean more than "Who am *I* to be the one to help free the slaves?" Does he also imply a larger pondering of "Who am I?" God answers him by saying "I will be with you." He reassures Moses that he is not alone. Ultimately God answers Moses with "I am who I am."

Could you say of yourself, "I am who I am?" The Aramaic translation of "I am who I am," is "I am that I will be." This implies that God is not subject to "becoming." God is everlasting: *was, is, and always will be* the unchanged and ever-present source, in a world of impermanence.

> *"...the boundless...infinite...It is absolute undifferentiation in perfect, changeless oneness."* -Daniel C. Matt from *The Essential Kabbalah*

To question God, and to question the self, dovetails the personal with the mystical. To know the *self* is the beginning of knowing God's presence. You will see this further as you continue to unveil. After questioning, you find a constant creative force flowing through you. It becomes prevalent. Is this the presence of the Divine? Is finding this life force a recognition of the Godly-self within? Dancing within the yellow veil brings illumination. It becomes elucidated because you are searching and asking as you observe.

Poignantly, the burning bush, although fiery and bright, is not consumed. This is crucial to creativity. Creativity passes through you, from source into art. It never gets used up. You become that ever-renewed burning bush. You become the conduit of originality. You are the burning, the fire, the question and the answer. You are God-like in your creativity. Creation happens in a field of conscious observation. Whenever you play in the imaginative realm, you heighten your sensitivity to the supernal.

As you peer through the yellow veil, glorious images of who you are, and what you could co-create begin to appear. Inspiration springs forth like a flame. As you create, something of yourself becomes evident. It is said that you are created in God's image. You resemble the Creator because *you* are also a creator/creatrix.

Who Are You?

"One can have no smaller or greater mastery than mastery of oneself." -Leonardo Da Vinci

Imagine, if you will, a vast array of galaxies dancing in an expanding universe. You look up at innumerable stars of pulsing light. Perhaps you imagine that there are multiple universes. Then on one beautiful blue planet, as you look closer, there you are, observing not only this amazing universe, but also yourself!

What is this self-awareness? What is this relationship with your own consciousness? It is one relationship you are always having. How do you come to understand the *"self"* and your knowledge of it?

As you look, the "Who am I?" question summons self examination. "Who am I to be observing this Universe?" In order to answer "Who am I?" with something other than your name, what you do, or a description of what you look like, you need to change from the material channel to the spiritual channel. You need to observe from a spacious outlook. Are you Kismet, a belly dancer, 5'2", 110 pounds, with long brown hair parted in the middle, and big brown eyes? I'm not even her anymore!

When you choose your belly dance name, as an example, you try to give a name that personifies who you think you are, and/or how you would like others to see you. My dance name, as mentioned, is *Kismet*, which means destiny— a once in a lifetime experience. More precisely it means...a force that predetermines what will happen next.

Choosing your own name is a distinctive act of self co-creation. The naming takes on a possessive sense of power. It gives you permission to broaden and heal your own self image. It grants women a step toward empowerment. It is not a name she is given, but a name she has chosen. There arises an ability to actually *be* this self. A shifting is then born that allows for change. What name would you give yourself?

Now, at this time in the dance, I am mentor. I watch younger more fluid students capture the legacy I was given. They keep the dance alive. The gift comes full circle. I am the mentor, the one dancing, the one watching, the Divine essence of expression and also the one dying. "Who am I?" begins to merge with my spiritual understanding of letting go into a unification with the everlasting Divine.

Who Am I?

I am the dancer twirling in orbit
I am the wind behind a leaf,
the legacy of my mother's mother
the daughter of soul.

I am the Holy One embodied in matter,
Love expressing itself over and over again.

I am the son of my father's father,
the embryo yet unborn,
criss-crossed chromosomes
rocking in seas of amniotic fluid.

I am the Holy One embodied in matter,
Love expressing itself over and over again.

I am the hands running through your hair,
or the sweet embrace of lovers;
Now, the purposeful creation and destruction
of a red star at night.

I am the Holy One embodied in matter.
Love expressing itself over and over again.

I am the thought that crossed your mind
and the one you didn't have.
Sensation running through your body
and furthermore your last breath.

I am the Holy One embodied in matter.
Love expressing itself over and over again.

Who am I?
I am the Divine Spark
Dancing with the Divine

I am the Holy One embodied in matter.
Love expressing itself over and over again.

-MZN

There is a story I'd love to share with you about the amazing dancer Kalae. This is a story where the observation of belly dancing changed her life by expanding self capacity. She was in the yellow veil.

Kalae by Kalae Kaina

Aloha, my name is Kalae Kaina. I am 35 years old, and from Hawaii. I have been obsessed with belly dancing for 20 years now. Dancing professionally in the genre of Tribal Fusion Belly Dance for 11 years, I have two dance companies that I direct and manage: Shakti Dance Movement and Devi Dance Company. As a professional dancer, teacher, choreographer, and most importantly student, I have learned so much through my journey in dance.

When I found belly dance, as a teenager, I was initially attracted to the inherent connection between the dancer and the earth, the beauty of the movements, and the confidence dancers had: an inner power I longed for. This confidence was beautiful, I knew I wanted it. As a teenager, I was coming out of a stint in the Hare Krishna movement, and struggling with women's issues prevalent in that community.

I am naturally out-going. As a teen, I loved music and socializing with my friends. I had a passion for retro/punk fashion. As a natural leader, I always felt secure in my life; however, due to circumstances, that was all about to change.

My introduction story into the Hare Krishna movement is quite a strange one, and not common I'm sure. A taxi with an older man, and a younger woman, pulled up next to a car full of my friends. They asked my friends if they knew where to pick up some acid (LSD). My friends replied that they could help them out. My friends jumped into their car, and from that point on, my life would forever be changed by their actions.

We called this duo, the older man and younger woman, "The Tweakies." To "tweak" suggests being under the influence of stimulants. They talked on and on about government conspiracies, alien abductions, reincarnation, and vegetarianism, among other things. My friends were like, "You have to meet these people they are so weird!" At that time I would say we were a group of delinquents who enjoyed drinking, smoking pot, and taking psychedelics; so, of course, these people seemed intriguing to me. They would drive by our neighborhood after school and pick us up, myself included, and take us for joy rides, get us high, and feed us their philosophies. I was 13 at the time.

As time went on, they started discussing Krishna Consciousness. They converted me, and one other friend, into full fledged Krishna devotees. I developed a love for Krsna and saw much beauty in the art and culture. We were not, however, "allowed" by "The Tweakies" to go to the Krsna Temple without them, or to associate with any other devotees. In their eyes, they were the only ones with "pure" devotion. Everyone else was considered pseudo-devotees. We worshiped the older man as our guru. I honestly didn't know that what they were telling us was a very warped version of Krishna Consciousness.

It wasn't until one of our friends fell into a manic psychotic state from being on LSD, that I realized what the Tweakies had been doing to us. They were with us when he took the drug. It was all so wrong. (To this day, our friend is living out his life in a specialized mental institution.) That moment was a definite wakeup call for me, and I was scared. I didn't know who to turn to, or who I could talk to. I stopped associating with the Tweakies. I was 15 at that time and very vulnerable. They didn't give me up without a fight. They continued to call and try to manipulate me. They had a master plan that I was unaware of: apparently they wanted to build an army of new devotees to take over the Honolulu temple. I was unknowingly part of that plan. I tried to go back to hanging out with my friends, but I was under so much mental and emotional stress I didn't know how to find the life I had before. My friends said I looked as if I was always on the verge of crying.

Eventually I went back to the temple; this time on my own. I met new devotees and made new friends. Finally, I felt that I could talk to people about my experience. However, in Vedic culture, women are considered a lower birth. Conformity to this level of modesty creates a feeling of being subservient to men. In my experience this became true for me. As women, we always kept our heads down, as well as covered, especially when we were in the temple room. We tried to keep our distance from the men, or brahmacharis, because these were men on a spiritual path who practiced celibacy. Obviously having women around, dressed in beautiful saris and bangles, was considered distracting to men trying to be celibate. Of course it was often the woman's fault if any flirting happened. According to the Vedas, women are seven times lustier then men. This was the customary cultural attitude. Not the best environment for my cultivating a positive body image and a healthy outlook on sex. If one engaged in sex it was only to be for procreation. If not, you were in Maya or Illusion. Much of the culture struggles with issues like this. I call it "the tortured devotee syndrome." You want to live a pure life and be free from material desires, but your body and your desires pull you in the other direction. So, you give in, and then beat yourself up because of it. It's a super unhealthy way to live.

At that time I had also fallen for a much older man; he was 32 and I was 16. This was also considered acceptable in the Krishna movement. I was happy somehow, and spent most days at the temple engaged in devotional service.

A friend and I wanted to learn Odissi, a style of classical Indian dance, because it is a dance of devotion to Jaganath, another form of Krishna that we worshiped. We couldn't find any Indian dance classes in Honolulu at the time, so we decided to start with belly dance. It was the closest to India we could get.

I fell in love with belly dancing immediately. I felt that I was a natural dancer. As I started moving my body in new ways; following smooth, round, and infinite pathways, an awakening stirred inside of me. I became comfortable with my femininity. Slowly I began to gain my self confidence back. I realized this beautiful feminine dance had been handed down from mother to daughter for generations. It had a profound power to shape and mold strong, beautiful, powerful women. Most importantly I began to realize that being a woman was not a curse or a lesser birth, but a blessing.

As I got to know accomplished dancers I met many positive female role models; this was something I'd never possessed before. As I became stronger in the dance, the process of leaving the temple began. I embraced doing other things I loved: like surfing and hanging out with old and new friends.

Belly dancing helped me transition from my very wild early teenage years: from being recruited into a cult, being influenced by psychedelics, or trying to find normalcy at a temple only to find myself in a two year relationship with a much older man, into finding my true self. I had also experienced losing my mom to Lupus when I was only 16. I thank the Goddess so much for bringing belly dance into my life. I really do not know how my life would have turned out if she had not presented herself to me.

Belly Dance was part of my transformation toward accepting and honoring what it means to be a woman. Realizing how truly powerful my body is was so healing for me after suppressing myself at such a young age. Don't get me wrong, I still have much love for the Krishna community; but in my experience, I have learned, that trying to adapt a Vedic lifestyle in a western world, seems backwards, and paradoxical. In relation to women's issues in particular, and especially for everything I have learned from our great western women leaders like Susan B. Anthony, Rosa Parks, and other remarkable women who have worked hard for our rights, I can no longer suppress myself. I long for expression, creative energy, and freedom. Belly dancing gives me these gifts.

Through the years I have come to know belly dance as my best friend. I can confide in Her, rely on Her to always be there, and I have learned that no matter what is happening in my life, what friends shall come and go, what places and people may change, or what ups and downs may occur; the one thing that remains constant is my connection to Her. She has taught me to love my body the way it is, and to embrace it fully. Body image is such a big issue for women, especially because we are so bombarded by the media's definition of women's beauty. I love the idea of redefining beauty for ourselves. I have respect for the American Tribal Style/Tribal Fusion communities for breaking out of the box and embracing individuality.

I am a changed person because of belly dancing. I take comfort in the knowledge that women for generations before me have been moving their hips to the same rhythms we dance to today: Baladi, Saidi, Masmoudi, and more. It is this connection, this lineage of women that have danced before me, that feeds my yearning for a link to the past, while I am still inspired to create from a modern contemporary viewpoint; all the while, holding on to the beautiful thread that connects all of us.

Observing your Life

If Kalae had not seen those strong and passionate women belly dancing, she could have missed her chance at freedom. If she had not felt their prowess, she might have missed the liberation ignited by shifting her view. She saw what was possible as a new choice. Instead of being maneuvered into doing someone else's will, she found her own free will.

Using all your senses to observe, you come upon answers that *"roll in ecstasy at your feet,"* - Franz Kafka. This practice, including observation of yourself observing, helps you lean toward the light. Even plants know to lean toward the light.

You can wake up in the moment of your life and really *look*. Here you find connections. You see meanings, synchronicities, hunches, and choice. You can move away from that which is not good. As you unveil the yellow veil, options emerge, ones you may never have known before.

Miriam by Miriam Groisman

When I was born, for certain reasons I will never understand, my mother saw me as a cast member of her favorite movie *Dr. Zhivago.* They named me Katya, like the daughter of Lara Guishar; like the Russian IKatherine; and to make sure I belonged to the Jewish community of Panama, they added Miriam, the name I go by now. Panama, where I came from, is located in Central America. It is a multicultural country with a Caribbean twist. You can feel the music everywhere you go: in the park, the street, the school. It's just part of the oxygen that you breathe there. I missed that beat. So, I decided to give it a try...to take the belly dancing class in the neighboring gym. I went the following Wednesday. I borrowed a hip scarf and went with the flow.

"My Gosh I can't keep up," I thought! The music captivated me because of my Sephardic background. The movements of the hips and arms reminded me how sexy I can be, and how much joy and pleasure I can have dancing by myself, or with other women; as perfect and imperfect as I am. Anyway, I don't want to brag, but I've still got some beat in my blood; "I can do this!" I thought.

In the middle of the class, the teacher calls for "circle time." Different women: the short, tall, chubby, fit, young, and not so young, all get closer as Meredith gives us directions for some kind of weird dance that we are supposed to do...an African one! Danga Boom boom Danga Boom boom... and I see how these women do their very own weird American stuff! My mind starts revolving at a million miles per second. "How the heck am I going to create the ultimate Zakuna batata African choreography and please this audience?" I want to die... "HELP!" My heart starts pounding, just like it pounded when the Calculus teacher called on me to say the right answer...to the bizarre homework problem I never had a chance to do.

I spot the water fountain, "Oh water fountain, you are my buddy!" I slowly drink the water that I don't need, until I feel someone waiting in line behind me. I stop my water sipping act, and sneakily change my place, praying that Meredith forgets about me. Somehow she looks directly at me, and my adrenaline starts invading every cell in my body. "Oh man." I do my show, and somehow I become possessed by Chita... even Meredith starts cracking up! The music stops, I go back to my spot, totally humiliated yet crowned as the new Chita in town. I'm still shaking. We break the circle and start dancing as a group again, but I can't recuperate quite yet from the African shocker.

Ever since I can remember, I have always been a very quiet, shy girl who hated speaking in public, or being the center of attention. I was too self-conscious. I was constantly challenged by my good natured, yet demanding father. He instead encouraged my potential as a competitor. He did not see my weakness as normal for a young child. I was the Queen Esther of the school. I was the best student in math, arts, science, and chemistry. In other words, I was the goodie-goodie of the family. But somehow I was full of fear: fear of failing, fear of disappointing people around me, fear of disappointing even myself.

Suddenly, I realize, from taking that dance class, just how far I am from accepting myself. That class touched the inner me: the shadows in my precious soul that don't let me shine. It is because I don't let go. The music that was supposed to make me be fluid like water, like truth, like Torah, like nature, like the butterfly, like the birds when mating... was just making me nervous.

Firmly, I decided that I would not quit belly dancing. My soul was screaming for help, and I owed it to her to pay attention; she deserved it. As time goes by, I start developing a sense of belonging in class. Together, we share our movement with different points of view: so different, so fantastic; each soul in different rhythms and colors...so intense and tender at the same time. There isn't any judgment; nobody is better or less than me, regardless of background or the number of years of practice. We have become sisters. We share a passion for mystical, oriental music that transports us beyond the point of letting go into awe...for the beauty of each others' souls.

Sometimes I still feel uncomfortable in the dancing circle, but I go with the flow. I'm not the same person that came the first time. I have grown in so many ways, and I can say very confidently that I have made peace with myself. I have learned that my soul is perfect, but my body is not. It will never be perfect, and that's ok. The perfection department I give to Hashem. If I don't start thinking that way, I better do it quickly... because I just found out that I'm expecting my new baby...number five.

Observation at the Beach

While writing this chapter, I decided to live what I was writing. I took myself to the beach. It was a quiet, rainy day, with the sun peeking in and out. In comfy sweat pants, with rhinestones on them, and a cool and sloppy tee shirt, with rhinestones on it, I sat down on the edge of the earth to "observe."

I watched myself perceive graying clouds. They formed a convex line pointing toward the horizon. I felt rain falling sweetly on my face and skin. The cooled drops, the same temperature as the air, landed on me gently. I saw the ever present surf in tiny versions of Hawaiian pipelines crashing onto smoothed sand. There were distant surfers enjoying the waves; all in wet suits, looking like seals. One was lying on the beach. I wanted to talk to him about how everything looked and felt so beautiful. Then an older man with white hair, also wearing a wet suit, entered the water, on my left. He had a pink boogie board. I had seen him days ago, enjoying the surf when it was much wilder. Then a seagull caught my eye.

There were many, but this one was chasing a sandpiper...unmercifully. I felt many emotions, about the rain, the surfers, and thoughts about pervious days. I sensed the immense beauty, and the sandpiper's plight. Later, when I looked left, I saw that the man with the white hair wasn't there. Had he left, did he drown, did he walk off the beach as he walked out of my mind? Should I be concerned? I looked around and did not see him. I had been sitting there for some time in a quasi-meditative state. Had I missed the entire scene with him surfing? What else did I miss? I took my time leaving, as solitude was coming to an end. What had I observed; the environment, my feelings, or the idea that God had perhaps given me more beauty than I even deserved? Thoughts of bullying birds, and time passing in waves, with people coming and going in and out of my vision made me wonder at the world.

As you observe, you envision. What you look at becomes changed. You imagine and conceive possibilities. What is happening, what could have happened, what will happen? How, as the observer, do you affect what happens? Does looking, thinking, and feeling have anything to do with reality being formed before your eyes?

Plato would have you looking at shadows on the walls, and Quantum Physics would leave you discerning between a wave and a particle. Aborigines would have you experiencing dreamtime as reality.

When I was in graduate school, studying to be an art teacher, we had many lectures on the nature of art and imagination; and on "What is Reality?" Those professors were on to something! As a creative being, created in the image of your creator, you also create, even by the simple act of observing. Perhaps how you observe decides much of your existence. What do you see about your own true nature? Who are you? Who is observing?

What is Arising?

Just as I didn't see the white haired man with the pink boogie board, you often exclude portions of what is actually present. There is an amazing *selective attention* video I would love you to watch. If you have never seen it, I don't want to spoil it for you, please check it out. It is by *Daniel Simons and Christopher Chabris.* Google *Selective Attention Video.* It is an insightful test of observation.

When you are in denial you don't see. Yet when you are into something, you notice it with greater frequency. Until my daughter was pregnant, I didn't notice how many other pregnant women were in my environment. Suddenly they were everywhere. How much of reality do you create, or miss, through your gaze? In science there is the "observer effect." It refers to changes that the act of observation will make on a phenomenon being observed. Also, the quantum Zeno effect, also known as the Turing paradox, is a situation in which an unstable, decaying, particle, if observed continuously, will never decay. Hmm!

What do you bring to the world by looking? What is the nature of your being that is displayed within this looking? What would you like to create? How does it feel to connect with that act of creation? I suggest that what you perceive is also a reflection of who you are. At any given moment you can connect to a much greater knowing.

Dance on

On this journey, when you walk, or dance, you observe. Consider how your life might have been different if you were born halfway around the world, viewing from that perspective. What remains changed, and what remains constant? Belly dancing may have originated half a world away from where you live, yet the perception of a woman belly dancing holds a universal quality. The belly dancer personifies "woman." Does her observer grant her certain unique affectations?

I have often felt that the viewer in my audience was dazzled and enthralled by the Goddess I was emulating...because they wanted to see her.

Do you want to see her? Perhaps you are her. Journey on to the next veil to know what she knows. Want to see what she has learned by embracing the "self?" Perhaps you will see how she loves.

CHAPTER 4

THE GREEN VEIL

The Fourth Veil: The Green Veil of Love

"Love has no other message but its own."-Mother Teresa

In shades from lime to emerald, Aurora Borealis, the Northern Lights swirl like veils over a blackened sky. Surely something miraculous portends here. Solar flares drape the heavens.

This is the green veil, with all the shades of a rain forest, a deciduous forest, fresh new grass, and buds about to flower. It is the color of sustenance. The root of the word green means to grow. Green is our source of life in the oxygen essential. But you are not at the North Pole, not even the land of OZ. You are in the green veil, the land of the heart. Like Aurora's magical heavenly light display, miraculous things happen in the heart. Forgiveness in the heart works wonders. Compassion can flower. This is not done with reason alone. You cannot live without the heart. You cannot grow spirituality without opening the heart.

Love Veil

Wrapped in the green veil you feel alive. Your heart beats to a rhythm that existed before you were born. It was entrained with your mother's heartbeat. It is entrained now with day and night, and yes, the swirls of Aurora Borealis. Feel the changing rhythms as the veil floats and undercurrents emerge. Like a curled green shoot reaching toward sunlight, this growing takes courage. Blossoming toward full spring regalia, you sense a change of heart. You need courage to dance with this veil. It has a force all its own. It may seem out of reach, or it may entangle you. Intrigue and yearning play with energy—and the beat of your heart. This attracts your eyes, your mind, and your heart strings. As the air catches your veil, like a curtain of northern light, you are mesmerized and inspired.

"Hope springs eternal in the human breast." -Alexander Pope.

There is hope because your heart longs to love. You are dancing with the green veil of love. Breath is totally connected to the heart. Each systolic and diastolic rhythm delivers the oxygen you breathe in and out, in and out. This is life-giving. Metaphorically, if you don't truly open your heart, you don't truly live. Here is a beautiful poem about breath and heart that my son wrote to me when he was just 19. It was his Mother's Day present to me.

2 My Mother…Love, She Dances…by Richard Ian Ries

She sounds Praise
She sounds Prayers
(4 dear friends)
A flower in the deep drowned Wood
There's Love in her hands
Healing in her Soundbreath
Hope
In a chaotic whirl
She is divine
& she is woman

Like Springtime Someday Mid-Winter
She is Change

Cleansed by Raincool shocking heat
Building...then Blending
Her new flame

The child in her has never died
Yet she looks upon life with expert eyes

I have joined many
Who follow her warmth
Seeking kindness & guide-dance

But I
(AND ONE OTHER)
Have Breathed Her! B4 my spirit knew Air
She is my Mother
The cycle and suckled mama of Life
Life.
Life.
& I BREATHED HER
B4 MY SPIRIT KNEW AIR!

I am amazed and always grateful for the sensitivity of his beautiful love. To have a son is a blessing. I cherish this poem and our amazing relationship.

But not all times in the green veil are so uplifting. Not all times in the green veil generate hope and beauty. You can hurt inside the green veil. There is a latent sadness there. If you rip the veil off, you won't learn about the sadness. You won't learn about the joy either. You might freeze with resentment. You could stay tightly wrapped like a clinging vine. You might be strangled with bitterness, and despair. This is not life-giving. How would you get out? How would you find safety enough to let your heart feel? Just how do you dance with the green veil?

Seven Wisdoms

- In *Deepak Chopra's Seven Spiritual Laws of Success* he lists:

  The Law of Least Effort, and Acceptance.

  You see that the veil of love requires acceptance. Eventually this acceptance becomes effortless.

- *In The Yogi's Seven Stages of Development before Achieving Complete Liberation:*

  The yogi no longer needs to carry out acts
  (religious duties) as he has attained the end
  of all acts through discrimination.

  Love becomes more than just religious duty. It discriminates between that which is true and that which is false. Only love is truth.

- *In the Seven chakras the Third Chakra is:*

  "Anahata," the Heart Chakra is the Sanskrit name of
  this Chakra. It means, 'that which cannot be destroyed,'
  the heart chakra is at your heart's center. The Air
  Element is represented here..relationships—the right to
  love: love, forgiveness, and compassion reside in the heart
  chakra. The ability to have self-control, and acceptance
  of oneself is here. Key issues involving Anahata involve
  complex emotions, compassion, tenderness, unconditional
  love, equilibrium, rejection, devotion, and well-being.

  The heart represents the place where animal instincts and spiritual advancement mingle. They form a knowing emotional intelligence that connects with the all-knowing intelligence.

- *In Lawrence Kohlberg's Stages of Moral Development, Stage 4 reasoning is described as follows:*

  Authority and social-order-maintaining orientation. Orientation to "doing duty" and to showing respect for authority and maintaining the given social order for its own sake. Regard for earned expectations of others.

  This stage is not easily seen as loving unless the care for others is implied by concern for overall society. Kohlberg did suggest a stage *four and a half,* which he called "relativism." Principles were questioned further. Past law and order, could there be a higher way or thinking about morality? These *four and a half* explorations suggest movement, past this stage, into a more personalized one. Perhaps it is a prerequisite to discovering a more heartfelt association with morality.

- *Dr. Clarissa Pinkola Estes discusses the fourth stage of love as such:*

  The Sleep of Trust: In this stage of relationship, a lover returns to a state of innocence...Ignorance is different than naiveté...
  There is an old saying 'Ignorance is not knowing anything and being attracted to the good. Innocence is knowing everything, and still being attracted to the good.'
  ...Relaxing into trust...faith and the power of innocence....
  rest in the presence of goodwill of others.

  Dr. Clarissa Pinkola Estes reminds us that there is a renewed perceptive in the loving spirit of rebirth. That to trust in love is to trust in the cycle of things dying and being reborn again. Everything is changing and transforming, ever evolving toward a higher love.

- *In Buddhism's Seven Factors of Enlightenment, the fourth stage is:*

    "Joy or rapture- piti... Joy happiness"

  For sure love brings rapture and joy. The body's wisdom is ready for that. When it reaches the heart, the mind is changed. We will explore what might happen to the soul.

- ***The Fourth Mystical Secret of the Veils: The Green Veil of Love:***

    Love Unveils Compassion

  When you love someone, you learn to truly care. You learn to give and receive with compassion. Have you ever felt a tree loving you? Have you seen its branches swaying in prayer over you, blessing you? Ah...it makes you breathe. Nature can help you heal. Sometimes the heart needs a rescue like that, or you think you can't breathe at all. Dance with the green veil. It is pliable. It holds the most essential mystery of all. Here you are being asked to open your heart. You are being asked to forgive the suffering that life brings and to offer compassion.

Experiential Dance Activities:

- *Veil and Rock Dance*: Find a rock you like. Now cover yourself with a veil and let the rock represent whatever keeps your heart from opening. Hold the rock against your heart. What feelings keep your heart closed? Then slowly being to sway or dance; feel forgiveness as you remove the rock and then the veil.

  When your heart is closed what is blocking it? Is there resentment, guilt, sadness, or anger? What emotions reside there? It is possible to find release right there in the central point of your heart?

- o *Give and Receive Dance*: Choose a partner and take turns dancing, giving, and receiving energy. Feel what it is like to give and receive when you dance...when your relate to another... when you relate to yourself...when you relate to God.
- o *Dance with open eyes* and look at everyone in the circle with love. Can you look with eyes of love?
- o *Call someone to you and then dance attached to them*: at least one body part stays connected at all times: What are you attached to? Is the attachment healthy or addictive? Can you experience detachments and attachments in a healthy way?
- o *Birthday Blessing Dance*: The birthday person lies on the floor and the dancers dance over her bending down to whisper a blessing in her ear.

  Can you forgive, feel compassion for, and actually bless another with all your heart? What do you wish for them? What do you wish for yourself?

- o *Drum solo* conversation...with drummer or with another dancer, answer each other non-verbally: When you "speak," what is your body, your facial expression, your body-language really saying without words?
- o *Goddess Dance*: Belly dance a *Goddess Dance* in the center of a circle. You are the Goddess incarnate where you can do no wrong. Everyone in the circle looks at you with love, as you look at them with love. When you perceive yourself as Divine, you can give and receive in a holy way. Can you love beyond yourself, your friends, your community, your country, the world of people, the planet, the universe?

Open your veil, open your heart, therein lies a treasure. Heart knowing is the meeting place of body and mind where soul resides. It is the meeting place of you and the Divine. It is the only truth with kindness. Come, peek inside. The green veil wants to dance with you.

Holy Healing Dance

"In many shamanic societies, if you came to a medicine person complaining of being disheartened, dispirited, or depressed, they would ask one of four questions: - When did you stop dancing? - When did you stop singing? - When did you stop being enchanted by stories? - When did you stop finding comfort in the sweet territory of silence?" - Gabrielle Roth

Belly dance is a healing dance. To heal means to make whole. It implies a gathering of all the elements of self, including the unconscious parts wanting to hide. When you embrace shadow and beauty, a mind-body-soul union forms. When you integrate you have integrity. You heal because you *are* holy. Dance can bring this knowledge. Ultimately, you must dance with the soul, not the body. The art of moving awakens internal calibrations. Your body is but a dense expression of Divine emanation. To know this your heart must be open.

As an adult, you may have stopped using the arts once you left childhood. You are then without avenues of completeness. When school budgets are challenged, the first subjects to be cut are music and art. Many never offer dance. This is cutting off part of yourself. You are denied that which revives you. This is one reason so many women are drawn to belly dancing. It is a grown-up form of artistic play that revivifies. It gives women permission to dance again. It gave me the physical, emotional and spiritual assimilation that would bring me to restorative wholeness.

While I was healing from a broken back and from my divorce, I created a mantra, a positive affirmation, a la Louise Hay. It helped me survive. It gave me peace of mind as I struggled with hurt and anguish, as well as a new burst of empathy for myself and others. It allowed me to find my heart. The mantra I created was:

"I am healed, I am whole, I am holy."

The word "heal" is a derivative of the word "whole." It is also contained in the word "health." To be whole is to be integrated. You are then uniting your whole *self* with the *One-self* that exists and contains all. Being healed is to accept the true essence of your being, the essence that connects with Divine cosmic intelligence. Here is how this knowledge came to me.

My story in the Green Veil: A Highly Personal Story

<u>Warning</u>! This discourse may be uncomfortable for you. It is a story of faith. With all due respect, if experience in the metaphysical realm seems only an illusion, perhaps the next section is where you should start. However, if you wish to brave the impractical, and trust in my commitment to tell the truth, by all means proceed.

It began during a difficult period in my life. I had just turned forty, I was divorced, my children were visiting their father, several states away, and I was alone, contemplating my life. Discontented with dating, I needed time alone. I immersed myself in books like *You Can Heal Your Life* by Louise Hay, and listened to a meditation tape by Beverly Kramer. It was given to me as a gift. It was basically how I learned to meditate.

Learning to meditate was no easy task for an atheistic fitness instructor and dancer like me. Sitting still was not in my vocabulary, especially sitting still spiritually. The only way I could meditate was in a bubble bath, with lit candles surrounding me, and soft music playing in the background. If my hyperkinetic body could relax, perhaps my mind would follow.

So here I was relaxing in bubbly water, attempting to meditate. Listening to the chatter of my mental reflections, I came to a realization. I had participated in much of the pain of my life's predicament. I had actually caused others pain. I was not the only victim! I contributed to a broken heart here and there. I even hurt my precious children by getting divorced and failing at love.

A rerun of my life passed before my eyes, like a ghostly Ebenezer Scrooge tour. The excursion altered my memories, or more precisely, revealed more accurate memories. I let fall some veil of previous protection. During this sightseeing journey, I began to see a great need to forgive myself. In biblical terms, the truth was revealed to me.

I saw that I had sinned. I chose repentance and atonement through acceptance of this recognition. Previous to this meditation, I thought I had forgiven everyone in the scenario of my life. Yet, without seeing my part, I had never forgiven myself. I had not fully opened my heart.

With humble yearning, I implored for deeper understanding from… somewhere. I asked for forgiveness for myself. I asked God, if there was one, to reveal itself to me. I asked for understanding. I prayed to know. I sought to find some unfathomable wisdom. As I opened to whatever it was that I was supposed to learn, my heart felt physically opened. It felt like soul surgery.

Light energy began pouring out of my open heart. Yes, I could look down toward my heart and see light shining from it! Crying and reverent, I yearned with all my being to become better, kinder, wiser, more open, more able to learn, and then it shifted.

I call it "the gifting," my "enlightening experience," my "glimpse of glory." Whatever I call it, it is never accurate, never enough. For it was not of this world as we usually see or sense it.

The light coming from my heart was sending out light, peripherally, in a curved shape around me. In a fish eye view, I became aware of blue sky, clouds, and trees. Yes, trees were very prominent and present for a long moment. I felt close to all things, one with nature. The connections feeling somehow obvious. Then, with a momentous force, I was shot into a great speeding light. Thrust into it. I was moving with this emanating, streaming, illuminating, fast moving light…at the speed of light…I was in the speed of light!

Then abruptly, it all became gentle. Here, a constant, glorious, luminous, all-pervasive light, within me and without me, was everywhere. Such magnanimous love was contained in this gently flowing luminosity, I could barely hold it.

Soon, my body could not hold this much love and beauty. So then I did not have a body! I no longer existed. I was one with the light. The radiance continued bursting with immense love and compassion. Words leave me empty trying to simulate this intense beauty, joy, and absolute awe-inspiring presence. The message felt, in unspoken words, was *"All is forgiven and there is only Love; a Great Love that runs the Universe."*

I knew that forever I could never doubt this presence. It was mind altering, life altering, soul altering, and I am forever indebted and humbled by this magnificence. How to honor it with my every breath has become my quest.

"Holy Moment"

Epilogue: The aftermath

After this experience I ran around trying to understand the meaning—literally. I ran to libraries and lectures, and I questioned spiritual leaders. I was sure there was an answer. "*What does it mean, why did it happen to me, does it happen to others?*" Of course! Literature and spiritual scripture abound with this kind of material. It is everywhere. Faith depends upon it. My husband Stephen, who I am married to now, once told me - "Every religion is based on someone's spiritual prophesy, connection, or enlightenment with the Divine. If you do not directly experience it, then you believe in someone who did."

When I went to a Catholic priest, he told me "Perhaps because you were not raised in a fundamental regiment of religion, you were more open minded, and that is why this was able to come to you. It is a gift of grace."

When I asked a Jewish rabbi he said "Who am I to judge, since Moses was talking to a burning bush? And because you have practiced being an artist (a dancer), you are more open to experiencing a transcendent experience."

When I asked a Buddhist monk what it meant, he said "I don't know what it means, but it happens to me all the time!"

At first I didn't believe any of these answers. They seemed like a good joke about a priest, a rabbi, and a monk! Yet, as the years passed, I knew they all spoke truth. I was not raised with religious training. I had been practicing transcending as an artist, and perhaps I was not to question why, or to feel alone in having had such an experience. Yet, to think that being a dancer opened me to receive this enlightening moment, has compelled me to share this with you. I keep learning as I attempt to live with what I know. I offer it to you in love, knowing that your path will be unique and precious. I believe that "God" will come to you in any form that you can understand.

> *"God comes to each of us in the form we can best perceive*
> *Him. To you, just now, He was a heron. To someone else,*
> *He might come as a flower or even a breeze."*
> -Richard Zimler, *The Last Kabbalist of Lisbon*

The Dance of Love, the Dance of the Heart

> *"All, everything that I understand, I understand*
> *only because I love."* -Leo Tolstoy

Dancing with the green veil is a dance of love. Belly dancing is frequently thought of as a dance of love. It is alluring, pleasing to the eye, inviting and mysterious. It is love at first sight. It captures passion. With all its glitter and bangles, it's designed to do just that, capture your attention, reach your heart, and make you fall in love!

Joseph Campbell, the great philosopher and teacher of ancient myths, discusses attraction beginning with the eyes. In his treatise on The Mythology of Love, from *Myths to Live By*, 1972, the Joseph

Campbell Foundation, he refers to "eyes reconnoitering," (exploring, searching, scouting) from a Troubadour poem by Guiraut de Bornelh.

> *So, through the eyes love attains the heart:*
> *For the eyes are the scouts of the heart,*
> *And the eyes go reconnoitering*
> *For what it would please the heart to possess.......*

Infatuation of the eye goes to the heart. That is why belly dancers are frequently hired to perform at weddings. The bride and groom watch the dancer. The bride sees the art of seduction. The groom heightens his desire. It is an implied initiation to union. The dance contains the prelude, the invitation, the practice of looking with the eyes to inspire union with the heart.

There was once a time in my dance career that I did not get past the invitation. I was a hungry tigress seeking spotlight as sustenance, instead of being a true seeker of love. Many current icons of womanhood are similarly hungry souls in search of recognition and validation. Watch current music videos and see what happens to the goddess with a small "g." She wants to be "seen" with eyes of love. She wants to be desired. She may be used to being the object of amour, but all too often she becomes a pawn trapped in the objectifying phase.

Love does not develop if you stay in the invitation stage. It cannot be just about what the eyes want. The heart and mind must be in sync with the eyes in order to create a love that can flourish. This iconic play of love can deceive with imitation. If you get stuck in a myopic view, you will feel separated. Union is not only about being desired. It is about opening the heart and desiring back. It is not about separation. I am reminded of a myth.

Love Story

Once upon a time, a very long time ago, there lived a forest nymph and a handsome man. The young man was so extraordinarily good-looking that women fell in love with him instantly—with just one look.

The forest nymph was no exception. One look, and she was hopelessly in love. She had just one problem. Due to her loquacious proclivities, talking too much, someone had cast a spell on her. She could not talk. She could only respond by repeating what was said to her. Her name was Echo, and the object of her desire, the handsome man, was called Narcissus.

When she met him in the forest he said "Come here." She said "here." She wanted to tell him how much she longed for him, but alas, all she could do was repeat after him. Finally he rejected her, and she pined away leaving only her voice to echo in the hills.

As for her handsome man, he did fall in love...with his own reflection in a lake. There he remained, gazing lovingly at his image. It never responded. It only blurred and disappeared with his gestures of love. He pined away also, leaving only a flower named after him; the flower now named Narcissus.

Give and Receive

What does this myth tell you? The two protagonists have unrequited love. One cannot ask for love, and the other cannot receive it. For love to flower, you must do both: give and receive. This is the faithful dialogue of love. It requires insight to give what is needed. It also requires that you are able to receive what you need. This exchange is clarified by compassion, sympathy and forgiveness.

In my work in mind-body polarity therapy, I see clients getting stuck by trying to be the *image* of desire. Staying in the embryonic phase, the fix of "love at first sight" is wanted over and over again. Here love is not allowed to ripen. Rubber-band relationships repeat a painful Samsara of attachment and loss. Or the story repeats itself with different players.

Sometimes loved ones get caught in what I call *attack and defend*. This is one of the major roadblocks to love. It only leads to more *attack and defend*! This is painful and repetitious because it lacks communication with compassion.

Echo's plight is calling for love and never getting it. She can never ask for what she wants, speak the truth, or express kindness. Likewise,

Narcissus's suffering, narcissistic self-obsession, does not allow him to find connection with another. Trapped in self absorption, he never gives or receives true compassion.

The ego's insufferable wanting goes on without satisfaction. You can't remain an object and be loved. You can't stay separate and be loving. You must come into authentic personhood. As you understand yourself, you can understand the one you love. This necessitates soul searching, and knowing with the heart.

As you perform belly dancing, you may start out being love-starved for attention, only to become a great giver of love. As you soul search, you learn that dancing is for-giving of yourself. It is not about being judged, or performing just to be accepted by others. It is about sharing the gift of yourself, the gift of your God-given talent, and the giving of your soul. By "giving up" your dance, you feel love passing through you. Side stepping your ego, you grant the audience just what they love. Joseph Campbell goes on to say:

> *In the various contests of Oriental erotic mysticism,*
> *whether of the Near East or India,*
> *the woman is mystically interpreted as an*
> *occasion for the lover to experience*
> *depths beyond depths of transcendent illumination…*

As in all relationships, the object of love can transcend being an idol, a projection of the ego. It can come into being the embrace of your dearly beloved, and finally into the love of all that is: the *"depths beyond depths of transcendent illumination."*

The belly dancer is what you will have her be. She symbolizes the Goddess of love in the ethereal realm. She personifies the one who wants to know you; the one who wants be chosen from the Harem. She wants to reveal her essential self and love you. She is a lover. She yearns for transcendent love. She is transcendent love. The yearning to know life, the Divine, and to know anything, is what is most desirable and loveable. You are attracted to that.

The universe is sexy; it's all about polar energies: positive and negative, male and female, attracting and repelling in a magnanimous dance of love.

Love is Natural

Love is natural. You were born in love, you are love, and what you are really doing here, on this plane, is remembering that. So when you open your heart there it is!

There are many anecdotes about this kind of knowing/remembering. Indigenous tales and mystical texts abound with this remembering. The great yearning for reality to know itself fires your quest. As you drop the mind and go into an altered state, you become privy to the deep truth that resides in the heart. Thinking and non-thinking become two ends on an infinite continuum. You re-discover or re-member One Love, One Mind, One Knowing.

Dancing helps you drop into the heart. It unveils hidden passions. Belly dancing jogs the memory that love is instinctual. The trancelike nature of certain moves invite reverie. In hypnotic sway and undulation, gentleness relaxes you into non-thinking. It soothes and inspires a letting go: like being rocked into sleepy dreams, where other things are born.

Become a Klutz

You become a klutz when learning grace. You falter to find. Similarly, your wounds and unfinished business come up when you enter a love relationship. Like entering the dance, all is exposed and humbled in order to reassemble. As a performer, you pass through shyness and fear of self expression. At first, your un-tuned body is trying to leap. So is your untrained mind. You fall, get up, try it over, and edit, until there is grace.

In the art of love, you falter to develop trust. You learn to honor one another and to declare yourself and your lover exquisite; not in spite of your frailties, but because of them. Illuminating vulnerabilities and standing in truth takes courage. Along the way, you learn forgiveness and compassion. Otherwise love is thwarted. Ultimately, in a happy love you give it all, as in a great performance. There is no measuring of how much.

Another Mantra I developed for myself while finding love was:

"I am loveable, and I am loving."

My "Second" Love Story

It all began when I was driving to a Greek restaurant for a belly dance performance. I got lost along the way. Being lost, I found myself.

In synchronistic style, I was on the wrong street, in front of a fitness studio that had a large "For Rent" sign pasted on the window. I had been teaching fitness and dance classes at a large firehouse. Luckily I was acquiring many students, but too many to fit into the space I had. Moreover, the fire house administrator informed me that he needed the big room back, so I had to find a new location.

I stuck my nose up against the glass to take peek. It was beautiful down to the glorious pictures of fit bodies on the wall. "Perfect," I thought. Still feeling the cool window against my nose, I said a silent prayer…*"Oh God, if I could only have a place like this."* Little did I know that what I would receive was of much greater consequence than this business opportunity.

Fast forward:

For seven years he waved and said "Hi, how's business?" I did the same. For seven years our businesses were next to each other at this location. He owned an interior design showroom and I owned an aerobic studio. On occasion we would see each other late at night while closing up. He would be outside his showroom unwrapping delicate art objects. They were carefully wrapped in bubble wrap. He took them from life-sized corrugated boxes. I'd be locking up my studio, bundled in a large sweat shirt that covered my thong leotard and tights. Maybe I had on leg warmers and a headband. One night, we had a long chat about our respective dating situations. He told me that a woman was pressuring him to marry her. I asked "How is she doing that, maybe I can try it on my boyfriend?" We proceeded to share thoughts and ideas of an unusually intimate nature about our relationships, our sex drives, etc. It left us feeling so uncomfortable, that we went back to waving and saying "Hi"...for two more years!

One day, in passing, I asked what color he would suggest for repainting my studio. After all, he was an interior designer. In recounting the story today, he loves to mention that I didn't use that color. Then he asked me out. I said "I thought you were with someone?" He replied, "I thought *you* were with someone." After determining that we were both free, we set a date. He was not a gym guy, not much younger than me, and he seemed conservative, more like a man than a boy-toy. Not my type! But somehow I said "Yes."

Our first date, at a sushi place, flew by with ease. We talked candidly. He spent some time discussing his ex-wife, and feeling comfortable with his honest and intelligent sharing, I disclosed some of my own story. Once again our conversation grew intimate quickly. This time with better boundaries.

The next morning the town mayor was scheduled to visit my studio in support of a fundraiser for the American Heart Association. There were decorations in place, a live band booked, and many expected customers; yet when I awoke, my eyes were puffy and closed shut. They seemed glued together. Was I having an odd reaction to sushi? Could it be from "something I didn't want to see?" A Louise Hay interpretation no doubt. He looked so responsible and conservative. He was so open and honest. He was direct. Being with him meant being with a real man.

Things progressed, the fund raiser was a success. He remained pursuant. We continued to date other people. When he saw me riding on the back of a motorcycle with some guy who would fit the description of a guy on a motorcycle, he asked me if I wanted him to buy a motorcycle. That was strange. What kind of man offers to please a woman like that? I didn't want him to get a motorcycle.

One evening when he called to ask me out I was having a particularly difficult time juggling responsibilities. I blurted "I can't go out, I have too many things to do, I'm running a business, being a single parent, and anyway there isn't any food in the house." He said "Come out with me, I'll take you food shopping." I was speechless. We went to the supermarket for our date. I remember laughing while playing catch with toilet paper somewhere between paper goods and sparkling water. Who knew I could be laughing at such a stressful time? He was such a gentleman that when we reached the checkout, he paid the bill. I was stunned again. How sweet, sensitive and perceptive. It was more than generosity or a grandiose gesture. I knew his kindness implied a compassionate understanding of my struggle. I started to take notice of him in a new way.

After chasing each other and running off, and then taking turns with either part, we moved slowly toward some sense of trust. We learned this trust through a series of mistakes. We continued to date, but not exclusively. We weren't ready for that, or so we thought.

When I offered to help him get into better physical shape, he hired me as his personal trainer. The yacht club condos where he lived had a security gate. Each time I arrived for the session, I was announced by the security guard before I entered.

One day I arrived unsolicited in the early morning. He had not called me for quite some time, not even for a workout. We were most definitely in the cycle of me wanting him. I was really missing him, and thought this would be a clever and flirty way to regain contact. Passing the security gate proved easy as I expressed my "surprise" intentions.

I arrived. The door opened slightly. He stood there in a silky dark blue bathrobe, tying it jauntily at the waist. I stood there in my headband and fitness clothes, and he told me he was with someone. Mortified I casually replied "Aren't you even going to ask me in for coffee?" I cried all the way home. I knew we weren't exclusive, and I knew I had arrived unannounced, but it didn't seem to help.

The next morning he came to my studio, two doors down from his showroom, and he was angry with me for arriving unannounced! The nerve! In the midst of our heated encounter, I somehow had the wherewithal to hear him say "I would have much preferred to be with you."

So, as I said, we took turns with approach and avoidance. I left love notes on his car, he sent me flowers, or one of us would be there casually hanging around after work. Nevertheless, it took us quite some time to get the rhythm in sync.

Another poignant day we sauntered into the Pizza place four doors down from our work places. The man swinging dough used to tease us and say "two lonely souls." We still joke about that too, but it was true. While waiting for pizza, we sat near the window at a small café table. I remember doodling nervously on the place mat stamped with a map of Italy. He asked "How would you like to be exclusive with me?" My heart skipped the proverbial beat and I said "Yes"...again. By now our bodies were longing for each other. The first time he kissed me I knew my world was about to change. Once while sitting in the car, he placed his hand on my leg and some really intense energy went through me. I became conscious that my body liked him even more than I did! You know my kinesthetic philosophy by now: the body is the first knower of wisdom. So our dating continued and we met each other's children. We shared holidays, school plays, dinners, and eventually he accompanied me to belly dance gigs.

At one Russian night club a man came up to him while I was dancing, and said, "How can you let your wife do that?" I was not even his wife then, but that must have clinched it for him. He did not enjoy being my body guard at midnight performances anyway. The incident sparked a string of arguments after dance gigs that sometimes ended up in love making before I was fully out of costume. Stormy weather! We had soul searching discussions about my passion to dance, and his desire to protect me. It was a challenging time. Although I had a full-time fitness business, and two children to care for, belly dancing was one of my soul's highest expressions, or so I thought. To be honest, many of the jobs were not of the artistic quality I had become accustomed to. I was dancing more for money than art; not that they have to be mutually exclusive. The stubbornness of our arguments seemed more a matter of being right! I know now that having to be right is a form of violence. Perhaps I read that in a Marshall Rosenberg non-violent-communication book. It's surprising how often we wish to be "right." We dropped the discussion for a time, yet after he asked me to marry him and be engaged, he brought the topic up once again.

Love does not compromise. It demands all, so some part of my soul knew enough to choose love over performing in late night clubs. It meant answering to the relationship more than to my ego. It meant following my heart's real desire. Stay with me here, because I am not suggesting that women give up their dreams, or succumb to another's definition of what is important to them, or to sacrifice who they are for a relationship. But at this point we were battling *for* the relationship. There was much that had to change, and this was symbolic of a willingness to do just that. We needed to make changes to support one another rather than just to defend our egoic selves.

Since the performances were not congruent with art, the principle idea of me looking like an object rather than an artist, was part of his objection. I was adjusting to perceiving things from his point of view... the bare beginnings of compassion.

Love as Spiritual Practice

In the book *The Second Half of Life*, by Angeles Arrien, published by Sounds True, she talks about the "crucible" of love. Note: crucible means a place or set of circumstances where people or things are subjected to forces that test them and often make them change.

> *"We begin to release our reliance on fear or pride to protect us. We recognize in our later years that the only way to come home to our spiritual nature is to express our love nature.*
>
> *We need to bless those who challenge us to love more fully, for they are great teachers who show us when we are open-hearted, full-hearted, and strong-hearted or half-hearted, in our relationships.....*
>
> *The strong heart aligns with courage and integrity and meets conflict as an invitation to creative solving....to develop a mature heart which expresses love with wisdom.*

...Many spiritual traditions teach that being in any kind of significant relationship with another person is the most rigorous spiritual practice.

This was my spiritual practice, my fire and my breath of air. It was where my ego burned in order for it to be set free. Both our egos underwent great transformation for our love to exist. We burned with humility and pride. We burned with the need to love and be loved. That became more important than superficial arrogance. We learned this through forgiveness and compassion, and we learned it over and over again.

Once in a fiery and frustrating disagreement, I said to him: "Oh Yeah, any man who wants me is going to have to go through fire!" He replied: "Oh yeah, any woman who wants me is going to have to walk on water!" And so we did! Even the elements transpired to bring us together. So I promised to give up belly dance gigs and focus on the relationship. Unbelievable! Over time our trust grew and it took a while for things to change.

Let me fast forward again...

We are married. I'm performing a hip hop dance on stage with my daughter and several other fitness women as the opening act for a body building contest. After a few contestants, my husband struts his muscular tan and toned body on stage, in a thrilling display of masculine energy. He wins the competition in his age group. There he was, my Italian stallion, in his little zebra bathing suit, with testosterone filled muscles and a look of intensity on his face not to be forgotten. We were exuberant with joy and celebration. But there was a nagging thought in my mind, something was askew. What was wrong with this picture? It dawned on me that the pendulum had swung in quite an interesting arc. And, as all pendulums are subject to the laws of the universe, we had to find the plumbed center. I went back to performing. A more astute and compassionate consciousness guided my choices of when and where I would perform, but I was belly dancing again in performance, not just teaching. In one memorable show, I danced for an enthusiastic audience while both my husband and son played the drums for me. The support of the two most loveable men in my life was a great delight for all, but most especially for me.

There were many challenges along the way, merging our families, our extended families, our finances, and all the other transformations that come with second marriages. Our relationship was no piece of cake at the beginning. I had two teenage children, he had a five year old, and we had experienced plenty of disappointment and heartbreak prior to finding our love together. We had drama, reuniting, more drama, and enough sexual attraction to keep us interested. We came to know sacrifice. We learned how to answer to the relationship. We learned that a force greater than ourselves was offering more love to our loved ones, as well as to us. All the humbling experiences that brought us to our knees, pale in the bright light of undying acceptance. The joy outweighs the sadness. The healing outweighs the struggle. The trust outweighs the doubt. The love outweighs the fear. But first there was forgiveness and compassion.

Love and Compassion

"Love and compassion are necessities, not luxuries. Without them, humanity cannot survive." - Dalai Lama XIV

There are countless ways to open your heart. Yet it takes courage. The root of the word "courage" comes from the French word for heart. The root of the word "love" stems from two Latin words: "lubet" meaning *it is pleasing*, and "libido" meaning *desire*. To forgive, and to feel compassion, takes courage, and the desire to please another if possible.

Permit me here to share a love story within my love story. It speaks of courage and love, and implied compassion. I originally found this story in an old quiet book store somewhere in Boston. It was one of those places, down the steps, that catch your eye and lure you into lost time. Musing over antiquated, leather bound books, gilded in gold, or too musty to open, I found a grouping of small dark green books called "The Little Leather Library." The first of the little books is called

Dreams. It is written by Olive Schreiner. She was a South African author remembered for her novel *The Story of an African Farm*, which had been highly acclaimed since its first publication in 1883. It was noted for the bold manner in which it dealt with issues of her day: agnosticism, existential independence, individualism, professional aspirations of women, and the nature of life on the colonial frontier. I bought the "*Little Leather Library*," and paraphrased this softer side of her writing. Here is the love story for you. I hope you enjoy it.

The Lost Joy

All day long Life was waiting on the shore of a beautiful beach, for what she did not know. She waited so long she fell asleep with her head upon her knee, waiting still. Then all of a sudden Love came from out of the great sea, walked toward her, and touched her. A shudder passed through her and she knew what she had been waiting for. And Love drew Life to him. And of that meeting something rare and beautiful was born—First-Joy. Joy played and laughed in the sun and delighted in everything. It made Love and Life so happy that they whispered to themselves, "This shall be ours forever!"

Then there came a time when they could not find the child Joy. They looked everywhere lamenting their loss. Soon, they found instead, a strange child with wide open eyes, very soft and sad. This little one did not laugh and sing so readily. It seemed to play more heavily. Yet when Love and Life passed through deserts and rocky cold places on their journey, the little strange child held their hands and brought them together. When they walked through dry and desolate places, the kind and gentle child brought them water. When they were lost, the child showed them sunlight where it was dark. The little child, never a burden, was only kind and helpful. So they walked on, still hoping to find First-Joy again.

Soon they came upon an old wise woman named Reflection. She could shed light from the past into the future. So they asked her "Where is our Joy? We have lost the child, and we have been looking everywhere." The old woman asked, "To have that child back, would you give up the child you have now?" "Of course not, they replied, how would we quench our thirst, how would we stay warm, and how would it be possible to find our way? We could not go on." Love said, "Let me rather die than lose this child."

And the old woman said, "You have been blind." The child you had as "Joy" is the same child you have now. You could not have carried laughing Joy through the cold, the rocks, and the desert, unchanged. The sweet warm tender child you have now is Joy grown older...the child's name is "Sympathy." It is the Perfect Love.

Sympathy, Forgiveness and Compassion

> *"Forgive and ask to be forgiven; excuse rather than accuse."* -Mother Teresa

Today you would probably use the word compassion instead of sympathy, as it is used in the story *The Lost Joy*. Sympathy has overtones of pity. Empathy and Compassion embody the same concept but with a broader sense of understanding. Empathy means the ability to identify with and understand somebody else's feelings. Compassion generally means sympathy for the suffering of others, often including a desire to help, but not always acting on it. There is large caring and passion in compassion.

I understand my husband in a much deeper way than when we didn't practice compassion. We rejoice in the privilege of being in love. We practice a natural gratitude for the love we have, and we tell each other with sincere compliments. What holds us together now would not be as powerful if we had not weathered those storms and shifted our attitudes. Now, in the presence of his love, even when I forget to love myself, his love keeps me strong. I know I do the same for him.

When the first inklings came about forgiveness, in the middle of an argument, I would wonder how he felt. I would ponder what pain *he* might be experiencing, besides feeling my own pain. I would see things from his perspective. I applied what I had experienced during my meditation experience. I searched out the love that was between us, instead of the separation I was feeling. This is how forgiveness and compassion begin. It starts by experiencing the other with all your facilities. It surprised me when he returned this compassion. Now I know that often what you give out is what you get back. There were also those times when he initiated the kindness.

Relating from just the mind will limit your love. To love is to put your mind into your loved ones heart. When you both do this, love arises with great strength. It is a blessing to have the compassion of another. It allows you to feel fear, and to meet that fear with love. The greatest barriers involve judgment and avoidance. It takes strength to sit and feel another's pain. When someone is suffering, you are more likely to want a quick fix rather than to stay with their discomfort. That is because it causes *you* discomfort. Seeing with sympathy, you encounter fear, especially your own. But if you meet it with a love that tolerates panic, you bring light to the darkness—the blue light, the hottest part of the flame. That which sends warmth even to the coldest heart.

As you offer to be with suffering, you learn to relinquish suffering, not only to one another, but to the Divine. When you say "Let go and let God," you are usually talking about a problem that you cannot easily solve by yourself. If you keep willfully opening your heart, love and forgiveness surface. Then you release the problem, and also your pain.

Perhaps I could not have learned to love again if I had not practiced forgiveness: forgiveness for my previous marriage partner and of course for myself. It is so fortunate that after being estranged, my first husband and I were able to regain friendship. Healing is satisfying. But if you are the only one giving the blessing, that too is a form of healing. You do not engage forgiveness for the outcome. You do it for the present release of goodwill and kindness. You are always given the opportunity to learn more about love.

Once on a vacation in Hawaii, where my son lives, my husband told my son that he loves me because "She is the woman I want near me when I'm facing death." I thought that a great compliment. The trust and compassion required at a such a poignant time must engage deep connection. Something to honor in my everyday living. Our relationship has come so far from its turbulent beginning, it is now a safe haven even in crisis. It has been tempered by the continued desire and dedication to love better. And even that is frequently tested.

"Forgiveness is not an occasional act, it is a constant attitude."
- Dr. Martin Luther King, Jr.

It is easy to confuse forgiving with condoning of behavior. It is not. You might think forgiveness is saying OK to an injustice. It is not. It forgives the person, not the action. It empathizes with the ones who get caught in the Samsara of harm. An awakened soul will do much less harm. An awakened heart tries to create healing. An empathetic heart learns to love. Forgiveness allows us to release the need to punish or want revenge. That can create more harm and violence. Forgiveness acknowledges the suffering of others and what may have created their woundedness.

You do not need to stay in relationships with those who violate and harm you. Yet, as you forgive toxic acts you release the toxins within yourself. This frees you. You know you have forgiven when you feel no more pain.

It is a process. First you feel sadness, shock, pain, anger, and more. Over time, being with yourself through discussion, meditation, praying, and introspection, you come to see how the world contains suffering. You see that many are injured by it. You see that hurt people hurt people. And, that you can avoid being one of them. Compassionate forgiveness heals.

When the sons and daughters of God forgive, the soul arises in holy sparks where liberation and love abide. Sometimes this may take several generations. As you forgive, you break the chain of pain. It is within you to love. You can dissolve anger and resentment through empathy. Dance with the veil of love and move toward compassion and freedom. William Fergus Martin says:

"Forgiveness is simply freeing ourselves from wanting to punish...
A more forgiving attitude makes it easier to develop wisdom...Likewise
a deeper capacity for wisdom makes it easier to forgive...Self forgiveness
is one of the most unselfish things you can do. Everyone around benefits
as you become less demanding, more giving and more forgiving."

Eventually forgiveness applies to all human dilemmas, all unfortunate events, all happenings. You begin to forgive your own fear of death. Your compassion meets a Divine presence that melts fear into love. Courage and kindness prevail because that is the only thing that makes sense in a transcendent view.

"The practice of forgiveness is our most important contribution to the healing of the world." - Marianne Williamson

The ultimate truth is love. So if you are not coming from a loving place, you are missing the mark. This is the original definition of the word Sin: missing the mark. It's like missing the bull's-eye. Love spoken, blames no one. It is non-judgmental. Love seeks to solve the problem with feeling, yet takes responsibility for one's own feelings. It requests what is desired and asks what others need. Love is compassionate, insightful, patient, and forgiving. It holds the faith that in time others will see the truth of love.

This kind of love takes time. Just like healing takes time. Like healing, it recovers old wounds and unwinds your tangled misunderstandings. Faltered and imperfect, it is still the best you have to offer. With patience great kindness can emerge. It becomes the new dialogue of love. Not just giving and receiving, but giving and receiving with loving-kindness.

"Compassion comes from the root words "to suffer with," and for that reason many people actually fear it…Compassion is one of the most honoured and saintly feelings because it marches up to the front lines of suffering and says, "Take me." In this giving of oneself there is a direct experience of pain, yet in the giving there is love…Compassion has the power to dissolve pain by not avoiding it, but by trusting that love affords the greatest protection. By discovering that there is a reality—love—stronger than any pain, you mount your strongest defense." -Deepak Chopra, M.D.

I love the famous Christian quote from Corinthians 13:4-8. It is often recited at weddings:

> *"Love is patient, love is kind. It does not envy, it does not boast, it is not proud. It does not dishonor others, it is not self-seeking, it is not easily angered, it keeps no record of wrongs. Love does not delight in evil but rejoices with the truth. It always protects, always trusts, always hopes, always perseveres. Love never fails."*

Now that you have danced with the veil of love into compassion, come, let your curiosity guide you onward. There is a beacon for learning something else. Where does cultivating compassion lead you? Do you dare to journey on toward higher knowing? See the next Veil? Please approach.

CHAPTER 5

THE BLUE VEIL

The Fifth Veil: The Blue Veil of Integration

*"If the soul could have known God without the world,
the world would never have been created."*- Meister Eckhart

The blue veil, the fifth veil, shimmers in the clear azure sky. Pale and ethereal, it then shades into a rich Lapis lazuli, a jeweled color, reminiscent of an Egyptian ornament worn around a belly dancer's throat. Then it shades to baby blue again. This veil changes from spirit to matter, and back.

When wrapped in the blue veil, you are dancing in the firmament. You are flying and floating. Yet your feet are still on the ground. You breathe on the veil and it shivers, like breath on words. It can move quickly then free-fall. Formations appear and then disperse. The blue veil captures your interest because it is many faceted. Like a shining sapphire both dark and bright, you watch and sense it's different moods. It is captivating and complicated.

Veil of Integration and Harmony

The blue veil is the veil of integration. Blending and fusion happen here. You have observed parts of yourself. Now you are called to calibrate these disparate parts into a meaningful whole.

Equilibrium with poise creates union in yoga. Inclusion of opposites balance a design. Like a well-compositioned photograph, a well-played symphony, or might I say, a beautifully choreographed dance, integration creates harmony and synchronization.

Morning Thoughts

Morning thoughts can be provocative. In a semi-dream state, your subconscious might be urging you to integrate.

Strange thoughts this morning at 5:23 AM, about Latte and her death. She was old and sick but did not die voluntarily. The veterinarian helped. It was sad and liberating all at once. The sweet memory of her lingers.

You don't understand how God brings death, yet you bring death. When you eat anything living, when you assist the vet in helping your beloved cat die, when you war, when you kill, even when you birth, death will follow. All the change and impermanence you live with demands surrender. You wonder with awe about this forthcoming fate. You experience fear and love side by side, the beauty and the horrible in wide display, the suffering and the devotion frequently together. How do you integrate all these dichotomies? Is it enough to just *be* with integrity?

You don't really. You slide back and forth on a continuum. The peaks and valleys become smaller. The range becomes more manageable as you make small choices in honor of spiritual discipline. You learn to "find your voice," the one that speaks with power and truth, the best that you can.

The word integrity implies integration. It is a practice that brings you closer to the One. Each present moment brings together the ancestors and the children, the past and the future, the forever and the now.

May I digress for another Quinn story? I am forever quoting my granddaughter. Please allow. It is an "out of the mouth of babes" moment!

We were sitting in a restaurant, my husband, Quinn and I. There was a large TV strategically placed within view. Probably playing sports. Stephen's gaze was captured. So he had missed what Quinn and I had been discussing. I said "Honey, are you present?" Quinn said "What does that mean?" I replied, "It means...is he in the present moment?" She answered "How can that be? The present moment is already over. And then it's over again!"

Hmm, I thought about that for days, and later came to a realization. The present moment is fleeting. It comes out of the future, into the present, only to become the past. That reminded me of the concept that God *is, was, and always will be.* Not constrained by time. So many great wisdom traditions remind us to stay "in the now." It is because that is where you find God —in that timeless, never-present, present moment! Ah, the gift of innocent childhood insight!

So it is, that within paradoxical opposing forces that you sit and contemplate possibilities.

Possibilities
day-night, black-white
north-south, heart-mouth
left-right, depth-height
positive-negative, death-life
man-woman
child

-MZN

Do you find solace in the opposites, or is it somewhere in the middle way? I've often thought that the antidote to fear is faith, to worry, a blessing, and to anger, compassion. It may be, but you must go through strange terrain to get there. You go into the place where both exist. Can you hold opposites and find balance? Your life story may hold a clue to melding polarities.

I see that your life's storyline is a metaphor for your soul's work. It goes beyond the psychological analysis. It embodies a poetic illustration pregnant with blueprints to solve a metaphysical puzzle. As you engage with the pure story, soulful meanings emerge.

Take a look at your life story. Imagine it as a great work of literature. What struggle does the protagonist experience in a repetitive way? What opposing forces are at work? What does the heroine need to see? See the dramas that inhibit happiness. Where are the paradoxical tensions?

A "narrative" of one of my polarity clients demonstrates this metaphor. She was beautiful, intelligent, well-practiced in spiritual discipline, and also apt to have raging temper outbursts from time to time. She dated a person outside her family's race and religion and subsequently suffered alienation and rejection on both sides of the relationship. The on-again-off-again nature of the bond was repetitive. It became obvious that her soulful theme required *integration.* In the outside life, it appeared to involve race and religion. On the inside, it concerned anger and her cultivated enlightenment. I learned much from this client. I see now that each person before me has a story which reveals the secret longing of their soul. What is your story?

In dance you use contrast. You leap by first pressing down. In belly dance you may push the ball of your foot into the floor to lift your hip. You might lower your shoulder as you raise your arm. You shimmy your hips at one-hundred shimmies per-second while your arms float up at a barely perceptible pace. You travel in a circle to come to know center. You surrender to the not-knowing in order to know.

You live in both realms, the material and the spiritual. Unseen forces of the mysterious realm intersect on this plane. They affect your life. You see how nothing really happens without the mysterious unseen forces. You find intersection between prayer and reality, between duality and oneness.

The word *yoga* is Sanskrit for union: to join the higher and lower self, the mind and the body, and ultimately, the soulful self with the Divine. When you do this you are still having a human experience. Being spiritually aware, still embracing human frailties, is part of the awakening.

At the blue veil, you learn to speak your truth and express your story. The mouth is between the head and the heart. You find harmony between mind and emotion. Your story becomes your truth. Your story possesses mystical secrets about your soulful self.

Here is Nata's story of melding in the blue veil.

Story of Nata by Nata Chantilly

I used to go by Natalie Phoenix, but I have changed my artist name to Nata Chantilly.

I started learning belly dancing 12 years ago when I was 20. I have always been attracted to the "other-worldly" qualities of Middle Eastern traditions. As I was growing, becoming a woman, these interests motivated me to take classes. The aesthetics of unique movements and exotic music really captured me. I began learning American Cabaret Style Belly Dance, then moved on to other modalities such as Egyptian, American Tribal, and finally, my niche now, Tribal Fusion-Style Belly Dance.

Having taken workshops with professional dancers from around the world, I have learned that Belly Dance originally came from the Indian temple dances. Through diasporas, theses temple dances were brought to the Middle East...where they eventually became belly dancing as we know it today. People continued to bring it further west into Spain, where it became Flamenco. Being very attracted to all these dances: the earthiness, the passion, and the steps, I also studied Classical Indian Odissi as well as Flamenco. Now, I fuse some of the movements from these different dances; however, the core of my moves originates from the pure classical style of belly dancing.

Isolation of body parts is particularly emphasized in Tribal Fusion. We train our bodies by practicing Yoga and Pilates, and also through repeated body-isolation drills. I have gained an acute awareness of my body, especially for muscle tone, through this rigorous training. As I trained, I came to learn many new things about myself and others. Through the dance I have met wonderful people, especially at dance event-workshops. People fly to one location, from all corners of the globe, to share the same passion of dance, and to meet each other. Here I have met other artists who understand my infatuation. Tribal belly dance enthusiasts, in particular, are exceptionally caring and sweet. Moreover, I have made wonderful friendships with the people that I dance with regularly. The community built around belly dancing, especially here on Oahu, is something we all cherish. It is one of the driving forces that invites me to continue dancing.

I have my life now because I discovered belly dance...and because I continue to dance. I used to be extremely shy. I was afraid to speak in front large groups of people. Through teaching and performing, I have become more confident...under my skin. Since I cannot show that I am nervous when performing, or teaching, since that is not professional; when I am nervous now, I put on the game face, and get on stage. The more I perform, the more I get use to performing. Furthermore, when I am teaching dance classes, I have to be precise in my instructions so that the group stays in unison: the angle of the arms, the body, the timing of the turn and so on, all have to be communicated precisely. These skills translate into my other profession as well...being a Japanese language teacher.

Dance, music and language all share similar processes. They require learner-progression and learner skill-sets, as well as progressive stages of acquisition when acquiring these skills. Dance, music and language entail similar proficiencies. Having to visualize and imagine the end product, doing drills, learning by observing others, and comparing one thing to another in a meaningful scenario, while interpreting and interacting appropriately within the environment, is also required. So when I create lessons in Japanese language, or in dance, I think of these learning factors, and I am able to come up with clear instructional strategies.

I have learned so much through belly dancing. I have learned about cultures, dance, music, art, and language from international cultures. Additionally, while interacting with this diverse dance community, I have learned to be well-rounded within myself. I have gained self-esteem and confidence. The artistry and disposition I have achieved, enables me to inter-relate with other artists and musicians. I cannot imagine what my life would have been like without Belly Dance.

You can see how Nata has integrated not only diverse dance forms, but also a melding of her talents that transfer from dance to teaching language. She even shares diverse ideologies across cultures in a way that strengthens her relationships.

The Not-So-Young, Not-So-Old Woman

Once upon a time-less time, there lived a young woman. She spent many of her days collecting flowers for bouquets, gems for necklaces, and stories for books. She loved the beautiful and the interesting. She searched secret places to find the best possessions. She didn't have to go far. Many treasures were near because she had the gift of sight.

One day she saw a morning glory both pale and bright. Its color blue opened to the sun. It seemed to bloom in glorious harmony with the light. She said,

"Flower, may I choose you for my bouquet?"

The flower replied, "I would have to leave my place in the sun. What would you offer me to do this?"

"Why, I would give you my beauty," she answered.

"Very well then," said the flower. So the young woman gently plucked the flower. As she picked it, it became even more beautiful.

Next she began her search for a precious gem. Near the entrance of a deep dark cave, a shaft of light revealed a glistening sapphire. It's gleam was so bright, it seemed that the gem was chanting OOOOOMMMMMM in the vibration of light. She could scarcely look at its splendor. It was like looking at the sun and hearing angels singing at the same time. The woman approached.

"Oh most beautiful gem, may I have you for my precious collection of jewels?" inquired the woman.

"I might mind leaving the safety of my cave," responded the gem. "What would you offer me to leave?"

"I will give you my gift of song." answered the woman.

"OOOOMMMM, very well then." The gem replied in a most pleasing voice.

So the woman picked up the precious stone and carefully put it in her velvety soft pocket for safekeeping.

Soon she began her search for a story. Not just any story. She wanted a sacred story. She listened to travelers and homebodies. She listened to ones who gossiped. She listened to braggarts and fakers. None of their stories seemed sacred. The stories did not touch her heart. A sacred story always touches the heart.

So she went on searching. She was about to give up, when one fine day, while sitting near a tall tree whispering in the wind, she also heard two children whispering! They were playing an imaginary game. One child was a King, and the other a Queen. Although they described very different kingdoms, from very different lands, with very different castles, they managed to fall in love and have a very fancy wedding. Of course they had to slay a few dragons, and overcome some magical spells along the way. Yet they united their kingdoms and lived happily ever after. Even their children had shining, happy faces that reflected their enchanted love.

The woman loved the story, including the scary parts. It reminded her of the story of her and her husband, the trials, tribulations, and triumphs they encountered, and the love they shared together. So she wished to have the story. She said, "Dear children, may I have your story for my book?"

"Of course," they whispered, because they were children of kindness just like you.

"What can I offer you?" asked the not-so-young woman, by now.

"What do you wish to give us?" replied the kind children.

"I'll give you my gift of dance!"

With that the woman began to dance for them. She held their little hands and began to sway, jump, jiggle, and leap into the air. She encouraged them to join her. She taught them how to tell a story without words...by just using their bodies. Much joyous time went by as they danced and danced, for dancing can lose time.

After awhile, the not-so-young woman went on her way. Looking less beautiful, her voice a bit scratchy, and her steps not quite so high, she journeyed homeward. Singing and dancing anyway, because she was so filled with joy.

Once in her cozy cottage she admired her treasures. She showed them to her husband who took a kindly interest in her sweet delight.

Strangely, she decided not to put the flower in a bouquet. Instead she gently pressed the most beautiful flower she had ever seen, for it had grown more glorious, into the pages of her book. Magically it sprang to life and decorated each page with a border of blue morning-glories embellished with golden leaves. The design repeated over and over again so that each page was outlined and delicately embossed.

Strangely, she did not to put the sparkling gem into a necklace. Instead she took the OOOOMMMM-chanting sapphire and pasted it on the cover of her book. Right in the center. It gleamed like no other gem she had ever seen. Then magically, it duplicated its sparkle onto the first letter of each page. It reminded her of an ancient manuscript.

Then, in her fanciest handwriting, the not-so-old woman wrote the children's enchanting story of the King and Queen carefully onto the pages of her book.

The fragrance of the morning glory permeated everything as she wrote. The chanting OOOOMMM of the gem hummed in the background. Somehow she knew the story would also have special powers. Magically it would have a different ending for each person who read it. And it would be just the right ending!

While feeling grateful for her book, she sensed a memory coming to her. She remembered the children dancing with her. It felt sacred and mystical, as if she were actually dancing with them again. The not-so-old woman was the old-woman by now, but she didn't mind. She felt carefree. She was taking pleasure in remembering, and creating her new book. The one she wanted so very much to share with everyone.

The End...or maybe not.

Seven Wisdoms

As you will see, all seven principles imply integration at this level. Here is how the other seven insights and traditions name this harmony:

- *In Deepak Chopra's Seven Spiritual Laws of Success he lists the fifth wisdom as:*

  The Law of Intention and Desire..."Intent and desire."

Clear communication to the universe in order to manifest any intention, must first be integrated. By harmonizing your thoughts with what your heart wants, you get the best of both. Intention and outcome merge.

- In *The Yogi's Seven Stages of Development before Achieving Complete Liberation: Stage 5:*

  The yogi becomes free of all waverings of the mind.
  The yogi obtains complete control over all mental processes.

As you learn to be with your thoughts and emotions simultaneously, choice appears. Then wisdom can arise. Self-control creates freedom through balance.

- *In the Seven chakras the fifth is Visuddha*

  Visuddha: Extraordinarily pure, the Visuddha, the throat chakra, represents the Ether (space) element. In relationships it indicates the right to speak... learning to express oneself and one's beliefs (truthful expression), the ability to trust, loyalty, organization and planning.(also hearing). Physically, Visuddha governs communication. Emotionally it governs independence, mentally it governs fluent thought, and spiritually, it governs a sense of security.

The idea of *speaking your truth* means speaking from the mind and the heart, with kindness. It asks that you listen the same way. With a non-judgmental curiosity. This chakra involves ears, throat, and mouth. Merging ideas from mind and heart come together. Many wisdom traditions spend a great deal of time discussing the sacred aspects of speech, and all that can come from harmful speech as well.

- *In Lawrence Kohlberg's Stages of Moral Development, Stage 5 is:*

Contractual/legalistic orientation. Norms of right and wrong are defined to laws or institutionalized rules which seem to have a rational basis. When conflict arises between individual need, a law or contract, though sympathetic to the former, the individual believes the latter must prevail because of its greater functional rationality for society, the majority will and welfare.

The caring for society, even to observe it as an extension of oneself, is the focus here. When you integrate your own behavior, you serve society. You are being asked at this stage to harmonize *your* needs with the needs of the community.

- *Dr. Clarissa Pinkola Estes defines the fifth stage of love as:*

Giving the Tear:....the tear of passion and compassion mixed together, for oneself, and for the other...Sharing future dreams and past sadness...healing archaic love wounds.

Here the lovers are offered the chance to integrate past and present. They are offered the chance to integrate one another into a relationship. They are asked to heal old childhood wounds of weakness and brokenness. Their own wounds and the wounds of the one they love. Healing lies deep within this integration. Love can mature and grow into a rare and beautiful state. The spiritual blossoming of balance deepens love.

- In *Buddhism's Seven Factors of Enlightenment,* the fifth stage is

Relaxation or tranquility- passaddhi, of both body & mind...tranquility and calm. Surrender personal will to Divine will.

This blending of personal will to Divine will is the ultimate integration.

- ***The Fifth Mystical Secret of the Veils: The Blue Veil of Integration:***

Integration Unveils Healing

To act with integrity one must have integrated themselves. Self understanding merges with transpersonal understanding. Intention and action work in harmony. Integration leads to wholeness, which shares the same root as the word *holy*. Only then will you be healed. Only then can the world receive the best of what humanity has to offer.

Experiential Dance Activities:

- *Center and off Center*: Someone with a strong attitude starts dancing in the center of a circle. The next dancer pushes them out and takes over the center. When it is time to assert yourself to stand for what is moral, can you take the stand?
- *Dance your shadow side*...witch, monster, scary demon...can you embrace all parts of yourself? Invite them to dinner, so to speak, and learn from the differing perspectives. First you must invite them in!
- *Dance as if you are a man (or whatever your opposite gender)*: Dance with imagined larger shoulders and smaller hips. What does it feel like to be a man? If you have a partner, what does he feel in his heart? Can you feel it too? Where is your awareness of the masculine energy inside of you? What strength does it provide for you?
- *Dance lying on the floor accentuating one body part* until all body parts are engaged. Like a baby discovering her body, dance until you can stand. Re-imagine how it felt to discover your body, one part at a time. You discovered connections of mind and body when you were small.

- ○ *Elements dance/earth, air, fire, water, space*: Dance like you are being blown by the wind, stuck in the mud, flowing in ocean waves, or being a flame in a fire. All these energies are inside of you as well as outside of you.
- ○ *Dance within the rhythm and then outside the rhythm*: play in and out of the rhythm. This is you in harmony as a follower and then as a leader; as one who goes with the flow, and as one who directs it.

Masculine and Feminine Integration

"To be well rounded individuals, we need to find graceful ways to move back and forth between "feminine" and "masculine" qualities, ways that allow those opposites to act synergistically."-Jill Mellick, *Coming Home to Yourself*

I marvel at my husband's affinity for family. We are in Maine. My stepdaughter Arielle looks radiant. I tell her she is beautiful. She encourages us all to raise our glasses in cheer. She announces to the two sets of grandparents, that a second child is on the way! My husband gets teary eyed as he hugs her. We are all so surprised and joyful. It is a forever moment. As I watch my husband's face reflecting the miracle of life our daughter shares, I feel his great capacity for tender love. And I remember the strength of my own father's love.

My father was a quiet man of laser-light wisdom and sparing affection. We had an amazing bond based on truth. He was shy about dancing. I got my dancing talent from my extraverted, affectionate, exuberant mother. However; one memorable time with my father leaves an indelible smile on my heart. And no, it was not the time we danced the father-daughter fox trot at my first wedding. I was stepping on his toes at that time. It was much later. He was very sick with cancer, and near death. I always thought of him as strong and fit, athletic and healthy. He never smoked and maybe had one drink a year, on New Year's Eve. I had come home to be with him at this time close to his death.

Being a professional dancer, I wanted to practice while I was visiting. It also helped me cope with the situation. So, I went into the large living room with music and zills in hand, and started dancing. As I glanced up, my father, in a herculean effort, was slowly and painfully making his way down the stairs. He stopped mid-way and said "I'm coming to watch you dance."

What sweet intention. Perhaps men bear passionate caring in a more linear way than women: what some have called solar-consciousness compared to feminine moon-consciousness. You may have noted differences. What do men feel of life within them, when it does not move inside of them? Where do men and women differ? Is there a difference? Some of the most famous prose, poetry, and songs are bountiful with blissful love, and are, of course, written by men. Do you embrace their loving tenderness? How can you love men more, and nurture their devoted qualities?

In relationship, women and men reflect both the weaknesses and strengths of each other. Eventually these very opposites bond to form empathic love. If men are from Mars and Women from Venus, then there are times they will just not understand each other. Compassion bridges the gap. Exactly because you do not always understand, you can care. The built-in difference is a Divine plan to foster sympathy.

Self integration mirrors this same complex and sympathetic paradigm. Whatever challenges arise, they serve to harmonize the masculine and feminine aspects of your own inner psyche. Carl Jung, the famous Swiss psychoanalyst, spent much time defining and exploring the anima and animus. Respectively, they are the inner feminine and masculine qualities of the unconscious mind. Ultimately, both aspects need to develop and mature in order to create a sense of wholeness.

Belly dancing, which emphasizes the feminine, helps to illuminate these energies through personification and contrast. If belly dancing teaches the way of the woman, then what does it imply about men? What does it say about a man's capacity to love you, and how you love them in return?

Belly dancing teaches that men love beauty. They love attention, and they love women. They like gentleness of hand, sway of hip and the mystery of unveiled beauty. Big surprise, you like it too! You may even like to be it!

By exemplifying the archetypical feminine, you are exaggerating what the masculine is not. It is not round and curvy by nature, it is not soft and pliant, it is not as gentle and receptive. You know this is representational, not a complete truth. But it is by this caricature that a peek at your internal "masculine" also becomes apparent. You learn about the masculine energy within. After incubating the feminine understanding, you are asked at some point to bring it out to the world. You perform your innermost feelings, and must find the courage to offer them as a gift. This internal calibration ejects your spiritual efforts into the outer world, thereby representing masculine energy. This can take many forms as you *father* your creative endeavors.

It is interesting to note that there are fairy tales, thousands, written about protagonists' in middle age. Many of them according to expert Dr. Allan B. Chinen, a psychiatrist from San Francisco, involve not young heroes and heroines, but rather mid-life characters. They are asked somehow in each story to assimilate masculine and feminine qualities. Usually the independence of the woman is evident, as is a kind of mid-life role reversal, where the man then becomes more sensitive. Self-reformation follows as the male softens and the woman allows for more assertiveness. This is mostly done with humor, for looking at the self often requires humor! As love relationships mature, the masculine and feminine differences recede into the background and the soulful commonalities prevail. This also happens internally within the self.

What other aspects of self are you asked to assimilate besides the masculine and feminine? Is each dichotomy actually a continuum? You may be asked to integrate the beautiful and the not so beautiful!

Beauty and the Beast

Beauty makes me want to dance. I walk the beach. I see birds fly over sea spray, as the unfettered waves undulate beneath them. They fly in never-ending shifts of formation. The art before my eyes is the beauty of dance. All is dancing.

Beauty opens the heart. This opening can even break the heart. Some say a broken heart is an open heart. Yet beauty opens the heart in an unusual way. The longing-gratitude of being blessed enough to witness beauty, is uncomfortable. How much beauty can you withstand? When you dance you create beauty, or perhaps, you play with it. It is already there. When you shift energies and play among the same vibrations in which birds fly and waves roll, then you feel harmony. Could it be that connection is what you call beauty? Could it be that you have integrated the self with something higher?

> *"On a very mundane level a dancer is beauty."..."*
> *Beauty is the illumination of your soul."*- John O'
> Donohue, *Anam Cara: A Book of Celtic Wisdom*

Poignant moments also come when a dancer is holding still. The tension and stillness seem to hold each other. Like a gaze between two lovers, or between a mother and child, the moment brings relationship. Primordial sensitivity exposes connection. Clandestine hunger is reflected in visible beauty, and your creative spirit yearns to catch a glimpse of truth.

When you dance, you play with energy. You play with consciousness. You play with the body. You play with the soul. And if you want, you can shake the soul loose from the body and for a moment see just how beautiful you really are.

This way of *knowing* is wholeness. It embodies, literally with the body, a holistic expression of who you are in the awesome dancing universe. You are integrating yourself beyond words, beyond logic, into the transcendent where all is One. Then you go back into the world and find the discrepancies!

Not all is beautiful here. Here, you have to bear the difficult, the ugly, the painful, and that which you do not understand. The shadow side wants to join you, not to take over, but to lessen its fears. Only by including your shadow nature can you fully assimilate.

In retrospect, the challenges of my first marriage gave me insights into the second marriage. They helped illuminate what it takes to heal. Not to include my "beastly" self, would be to ignore fears and faults.

How would I heal them without knowing them? Ignoring your shadow side will leave you unbalanced and wanting. To embrace that which is seemingly unacceptable can lead to acceptance and forgiveness. There is always the chance for healing to arrive.

Any emotion will reveal the possibility of new knowledge. When fear exposes danger, do you listen, or do you hide and never get the message? When ego rears its ugly head, do you see what is there? If not, it will rule you. If you push away the beast, you won't receive the message. Sometimes it is wonderful to dance like you are terribly ugly, to dance like you are a wicked witch, to dance like you are awful, just to know, on a visceral level, what lurks inside of you. This offers wholeness. Art is therefore not always beautiful. But it is true. What happens when you feel sad?

Sadness Integrated

You may wish to avoid sadness. But then you will not understand it. If you find a way to allow it to *be,* you can learn from it. There were times in my dance career that I had to perform when I was sad. "The show must go on" isn't just a motto. It became one of the ways I learned to genuinely feel and accept my emotions.

Imagine thinking: *I have to go to work, just like everybody else, yet in this job, I have to push my deepest feelings aside and provide entertainment for others. I must get into the car and drive to the happy environment of music and dance, yet my soul is crying. How can I drag my body filled with remorse, pain, and suffering, to this place, and then become the entertainment which brings happiness and meaning to others?*

I begin by going through the motions. I get dressed, bring the costumes, put on the eye make-up. Next thing I know, I am on stage. The music is rocking me, the lights are warm, and the audience, enraptured, is witnessing. Here I can melt into feeling. They feel it too. I give sway to my emotions. The dance has room for all my emotions.

Dancing while sad offers a remarkable opportunity for peak performance. People don't generally come to watch sad belly dancers. They save that for *Swan Lake* or other stories with tragic wings. In belly dancing they want happiness. Yet portions of the dance aptly welcome grief. They seem designed to hold it. Floor work and Chiftitelli, for example, provide a languid lethargy that can embrace sorrow. They hold elemental life experience with grace. The steps include a melancholy writhing distinctly different from an exuberant drum solo.

The word *writhing* means "to feel a strong emotion, to make violent and rolling movements with the body, especially as a result of severe pain." Undulating artistically, becomes an apropos representation of sadness. There were times I endured heartrending moments as I danced. They served to make my performance authentic. That made it universal. It also made *me* feel better. The art of feeling is healing.

Befriending your emotions is a great step toward integration. The process frequently needs refining. There are layers of understanding.

Now, please allow me to skip ahead many years:

Up in the middle of the night for no reason I could fathom, strange long forgotten memories reminded me of advice from the Dalai Lama. He suggests that if you live a good life, your memories will be more pleasant in old age. Of course, none of us have only good memories, and in any case, those aren't the ones that come back to you in the middle of the night! This memory was about me seeing my young son, maybe 4 or 5 years old, finding the bunny I put out on the back porch, dead in its cage. I think it may have died from being overheated. I had put it on the back porch thinking it needed some sweet fresh air.

Now, a stinging pain in my heart arises. In ignorance my good intention was ill-fated. I don't remember anything about what we did, did we bury it? Did we mourn? Why keep an animal in a cage anyway? What I do remember is my little son's slumped shoulders, and a palpable deflation of his entire body, as he said "Lisa will be so sad." It was his sister's bunny, and *his* first sight of death. His words were words of compassion. Perhaps some denial of his own pain was included, yet he was caring about his sister. Today he is a psychologist.

Where was my mind when I put the bunny outside? Why wasn't I more present to the possible danger? How was I so preoccupied? Was I in an ego-oriented-self-oblivion? This *does* shift through time and awareness! I do not ignore things so easily now that I am older. Yet self-forgiveness comes in layers. We do it over and over again. Even in the middle of the night. Especially when sad memories come forth. It is a major part of integrating the past with the present. It is part of accepting your whole self. But why did these flashes of memory come now?

Did my cat snuggling me remind me of the bunny? Was it the lecture I heard about self-forgiveness? Was it perhaps because my birthday is coming and that calls for a life review...once again!

How to have compassion for my own sadness reminds me that I had two kids, a dog, a cat, a bunny and turtles to watch. I had stress concerning a forthcoming divorce, and I was dancing into distraction to kill my pain.

What now? Do I practice enough compassion now? What part of me is still ignorant? Usually where there is pain, denial likes to tag along! Usually where there is pain, something needs to change.

It was not until later that I remembered why this bygone memory was visiting me? I had watched a movie about animal abuse. It was a story of a pit bull set on fire. Disturbing to say the least! It took me a while to make the connection between that movie and my sweet lost-bunny memory. I could not immediately face it. Not in full consciousness. That is why meditation and introspection can be so essential to a conscious life. It gives voice and time to that which you may otherwise skip.

As a dancer you are likely to examine your inner landscape. You find lighthouses of sensation along the way. You are fine-tuned to feeling. You travel past denial into sadness, or any emotion, into your body and mind. All the memories, dreams, and reflections, to coin a term, are there for the mission of incorporation.

What felt-sense is awakening in you for further investigation? Invite your shadow side and welcome your regrets along this journey. Find forgiveness for yourself. You cannot forgive that which you do not see. Every part is a piece of the puzzle, a holon of a hologram, a meaningful message for you. It is the story of your soulful development.

Maya Angelou says:

> *"I don't know if I continue even today, always liking myself. But what I learned to do many years ago was to forgive myself. It is very important for every human being*

to forgive herself or himself because if you live, you will make mistakes- it is inevitable. But once you do and you see the mistake, then you forgive yourself and say, 'Well, if I'd known better I'd have done better,' that's all. So you say to people who you think you may have injured, 'I'm sorry,' and then you say to yourself, 'I'm sorry.' If we all hold on to the mistake, we can't see our own glory in the mirror because we have the mistake between our faces and the mirror; we can't see what we're capable of being. You can ask forgiveness of others, but in the end the real forgiveness is in one's own self. I think that young men and women are so caught by the way they see themselves. Now mind you. When a larger society sees them as unattractive, as threats, as too black or too white or too poor or too fat or too thin or too sexual or too asexual, that's rough. But you can overcome that. The real difficulty is to overcome how you think about yourself. If we don't have that we never grow, we never learn, and sure as hell we should never teach." -from an interview with the Teen Talking Circles Project 2004

Without sadness there would be less soul searching, and thus no forgiveness. Without forgiveness, there would be no healing. Integrating means to include the uncomfortable, the ugly, the rejecting, and the ego, along with the beautiful and joyous. Embrace it all as you move toward self acceptance. It will help you accept others.

Here is lovely Patty's story of dancing with feeling.

Dancing Through the Storm by Patty Maraldo

Life is not about waiting for the storm to pass. It is about dancing through the storm. I have always returned to the ballet barre for solace and for peace. As a young dancer, technique class and performance development were most compelling. Dance was purely physical and always had to be beautiful --almost ethereal. My technique and physical appearance were paramount and impeccable. It was grueling, not particularly enjoyable and an outlet to push away or hide from stress, unhappiness and dissatisfaction. Hours of classes and rehearsals were my stratagems for detachment. Actual performance left me with a void that I could not understand. I felt only emptiness while my colleagues remained animated and exuberant for hours and sometimes days after a show. More recently, dance has assisted me in finding a deeper connection as to who I am within my relationships and my community. It has provided a return to my roots and a clearer understanding of how I want my life to unfold. In my late forties, I returned to performance. For the first time every fiber of my being was on the stage. I was in control of every micro-movement drawing from a skill and sophistication that I had not encountered before. I continue to find myself growing luxuriantly as I continue to find my way dancing through the storm, the raindrops, the rainbows and the sunshine.

Self -Judgment and External Criticism

One of the main contributors to thwarted integration is judgment. The kind from others, and the kind from your own inner critic. How do you integrate doubt and faith? When is looking into yourself an introspective exercise and when does it become a crippling self-rejection? Sometimes you have to stand up to your own doubts, as well as the criticism of others.

Oftentimes artists, sensitive trend setters, find themselves too much on the fringe of society to be accepted. Stories abound in the art world that tell of artists whose works have been misunderstood. They have been critiqued and torn apart by negative judgment. Then in a twist of fate, their words or paintings go on to become world famous! Many are acclaimed only after death. Perhaps it takes time for society to catch up to the artist's perspective.

So how do you know when judgments are helpful and when they are destructive? Are you motivated by fear of not being good enough, guilt of being wrong, or shame of having faltered? These emotions serve as guideposts. You are not meant to stay in states of sadness and self-recrimination. These feelings are only the tools. Questioning can be good, but too much judgment can negate the creative process. The progression that leads toward enlightenment is ultimately kind. One belly dancer, a notable psychologist from New York city, tells us a story of looking within to find answers.

On Combating Negative Judgments about Belly Dancing
by Dr. Ellen Haimoff

The inspiration for my poem happened about a year ago, when my fellow belly dancers and I were rehearsing a beautifully choreographed and original dance, to be performed at the local private high school. The dance was elegant – we were to wear white flowing outfits while holding bags of flowers; no skin showing. No undulations (rolling of the stomachs and hips) were allowed. We were to be carefully observed.

A committee of ladies arrived to see how we were progressing. But, really they wanted to see if the dance was "appropriate" for the young women of their school.

With stern faces, they asked us to cut out "this," and lessen the flow of "that." Three times we repeated the dance, each time cutting out more and more soul from the dance, and ultimately from our hearts! Finally, after tears and humiliation, we withdrew from the recital.

For me, the dance was a celebration of femininity, of joy, and of elegance. Our group has been dancing/studying together for about ten years. Each choreographed movement was infused with love, with sisterly bonding and graceful self-expression.

It is a shame that the school marms couldn't see beyond the "name" – Belly-Dancing, and had pre-judged us as vulgar and seductive. Perhaps they were frightened by their own sexuality and wanted to repress any element of that in their school of proper "young ladies."

Here is the poem that I created after this experience, and P.S. we got to perform the dance at a known off-Broadway theatre in Manhattan.

THEY & THEM

Who Are these Oppressors: "They & Them"
Who are everywhere and nowhere?
These are the people we empower with what
they say and what has been said
To penetrate our thoughts...a chorus of
Judgments ruminating in our head.
They spit, they sputter, turning hope to Bile
They pick, they putter, trampling our style.
What's wrong with "that?" What's up with "this?"
Their eyes imply "not good enough," and we're dismissed:
a wave of hand, a disdainful kiss.
Yet, we pay homage to our perpetrators of Yesterday & Tomorrow
They burrow deep inside us in a pit of molten sorrow.
In a cauldron pot they dwell,
their Talons, like the Flames from Hell.
Imposters of my mind...Dragons & Demons & Horrible "What Ifs"
I am the defender, & they are the Plaintiffs.
Oh yes "They & Them," Masters of my Misery,
You are Empty & Meaningless,
Unless I give you Usury!
-Dr. Ellen

Sometimes your inner critic stifles your expression, making you feel "less than" or wrong. Sometimes it serves you to help make an improvement. When you can see both sides, you find balance.

Disquieted feeling, suggesting that you are missing a part of yourself, may actually help you discover some dormant treasure. This is what happened to another dancer, Rosangel, because she followed her unease.

Rosangel Perez is a Spiritual Movement Coach and founder of Soulfuldance which hosts gatherings and events. She is also the host and creator of a blog talk radio show called Cafecito Break. I have had the pleasure of being on her show. Her conversation is charming and inspiring. She says her initiation into belly dancing was prompted by an awakening of the *sleeping self*. Someone you may have heard of inspired her.

Confessions of a Soulfuldancer by Rosangel Perez

*It started with belly dancing…*About 13 years ago I started feeling the itch to dance again. My body was craving movement. I was also searching for the rush I would feel whenever I would go out dancing, which was practically every weekend during my high school and college years. That is when I decided to take a dance class.

I was interested in perfecting my partner salsa dancing, but I didn't have a boyfriend or male friend, at the time, interested in taking lessons with me. I thought about the possibility of finding a partner in class, but that didn't appeal to me either. From there, I began considering classes for the "solo" dancer. Strip tease classes sounded sexy, but I wasn't ready for that. I liked Flamenco, but it wasn't calling me either. Hula Dancing was a closer option, but it wasn't fully connecting with me.

During that time I was working as a Production Assistant at VH-1 and was given the wonderful opportunity to work on *"Shakira, MTV Unplugged."* I remember watching this beautiful goddess…performing barefoot, and with no makeup. She was wild, free, expressive, and passionate on stage. I was instantly drawn to her. I watched as she rehearsed her set. When she began to perform *"Ojos Asi,"* I was captivated by the way she moved her body. It was sensual, confident, playful, and seductive. I was instantly in love with the art form and grateful for experiencing a piece of it through Shakira. This was my official introduction to belly dancing.

Shortly after, I began taking lessons with a beautiful Belly Dancer named Nadia Moussa at Lotus Music and Dance in NYC. The class was filled with women of different ages, backgrounds, and body types. It felt beautiful to be in this space. Nadia moved with so much grace and sensuality, that dancing alongside her, with these other women felt empowering. We were dancing for no one else but ourselves. It wasn't a competition. It was not about who could move better, who was more fit, who was younger, or prettier. It was an expression of love. It was the art of embracing ourselves and our bodies. It was freedom to be expressive. It was permission to be sensual. I knew I was home.

What began as a desire to take dance classes had transformed into a practice that is now a big part of my life. I call it Soulfuldancing. It would mark the beginning of a journey for self-love, healing, acceptance, and uninhibited self-expression.

For the goddess, the sacred feminine, for sisterhood, my higher self, guides, for all the parts of me past, present, and future - Thank you for the gift of this ancient, sacred dance and for the mysteries that are yet to be revealed.

Adoring Eyes, Belly Dancing, and Parenting Your Inner Child

Oftentimes, you may not see the *sleeping self,* the judgmental self, or even the beautiful self. Embracing the beautiful is as challenging as embracing the shadow. Adoring yourself may actually feel foreign!

There is reluctance at being adored. In love relationships, *being* loved can be an uncomfortable experience. Receiving love is a challenge. You must feel worthy. Self-love can bring a similar dilemma.

You might wish to start by loving your inner child. Various healing techniques like guided meditation, therapy, or body-work, can help. Although it's seemingly impossible to go back to childhood, you can use your imagination. Envision peeking into the window of your childhood home. What images would you see? How did the adults look at you? How would you like them to look at you?

In belly dance class, when a dancer is in the center of a sacred circle, they are privileged to see adoring eyes watching them. It's one of the rules of my class, to love the dancer in the middle. It reminds me of a baby doing cute things while the parents watch. The parents enjoy the slightest movement or sound. See a baby in a high chair banging her little hands on the tabletop and then clapping with glee. Now imagine the parents watching, smiling, and even imitating the child. This delights the child so much. And, the parents are off-the-charts with happiness!

To be seen with loving eyes is one of the strongest affirmations of love. To be mirrored is to validate that love. How often do you look upon another with love in your heart? Celebrate Divinity within someone, and you celebrate yourself. Spend a day looking into other people's eyes searching for the Divine spark. Then try seeing that in your own eyes when you look in the mirror.

Early on, when the dancer is performing in the center of a circle, after she overcomes the initial shock, she seems to be saying "Regard me, notice me. Here I am, do you see me?" Later in her development, as the egoic self becomes incorporated, it becomes "My soul is loving you when I'm dancing? I want to share that love with you. I'm seeing *you* with love." That is connection, and therefore beauty. It allows the judging-self to meet the Divine-self, where no judgment exists.

Babies are very joyful about being noticed. They crave connection unselfconsciously. You become self-conscious as you become aware of judgment. It's a shift reminiscent of the fall in the Garden of Eden. All of a sudden you are naked.

As you combine the need to be seen as your genuine self, with the desire to connect with others, you sense Divine eyes adoring you. A holy healing Divine universe is loving you. And it feels good when it passes through you.

I once had a mind-body polarity client who had a nice family, a creative job, good health, wealth even. Yet a nagging dissatisfaction kept him from true contentment. He told me that his mother never looked at him kindly, or with love. She seemed to have a perpetual scowl on her face. She was not punitive, mean, or neglectful. She just never seemed happy to see him. He was plagued with anxiety and wanted to find a way to be happy. In therapy we eventually worked on compassion for his mother. Why didn't she smile? It became clear that *he* had not denied her happiness, *she* was unhappy. This awareness took time. As he ventured toward forgiveness his own happiness began to awaken.

I was left with an indelible image: that of a parent not being able to smile, or look at his or her child with love. Such a subtle gesture of happiness was missing.

It is a gift to become a parent. Babies bring love. Sometimes you get so caught up in the responsibility of another life, you forget to notice the innate joy the child is giving you. When you look into their eyes you can see unconditional love. You were born that way.

How to Adore:

If you received adoring eyes as a child, you were privileged. Perhaps you can give that gift to others now. If I could give that gift to every inner child, here is the ideology for passing that on. Apply this generously to your self-love! And to your children, if you are so blessed.

Remember that your child is irreplaceable in the entire cosmos. What if you could look adoringly at your own inner child, as well as the children around you? Parenting is about receiving as much as it is about giving. Receive your child's pure love. Watch your child unfold and become who they are. This is more important than trying to make the child who you want them to be. Parenting will teach you about yourself. Imagination supersedes discipline every time. Use the child's natural curiosity and love of imagination to guide them. Force creates backlash, creativity is better. Teach the art of compromise. Avoid power struggles; life is ultimately more about making your own rules rather than following someone else's. Children learn what they see, take good care of yourself. The best form of discipline for children is the parent's practice of self discipline. And, if it's not kind don't do it! Love your spouse/partner: this is one of the best gifts you can give your child. Keep your sense of humor as you practice patience and compassion. You'll need it. Your child's concept of God will likely come from how you raise them. How do you want the Source of creation to be viewed by them? Imagine yourself as your own parent….would you like to have yourself as a parent? Speak words in the positive…try to avoid "no" and "don't"; offer invitation instead. Learn about child behavior and age appropriate challenges, and share ideas with other intelligent people. Have fun and learn to play again. Forgive yourself when you make a mistake, and forgive your child. Love involves forgiveness. Look at your child with adoring eyes. They remember God better than you do. See the divinity in their eyes. -MZN

Raising children is more art than science. We play with half of ourselves and half of our loved one, in a never-before-seen creation of love. Even if the child does not come from your blood line they will love you just the same.

I can see life for the third time in my lifetime. First my own, then my children, and now my grandchildren. It's a task both fragile and sturdy. No wonder we don't live longer. If I lived 200 years I could not catch up to the growth spurt of consciousness my grandchildren will bring. How much better it is to give new notions to the new people. In that case we must treat them with great love. And oh yes, look at them with adoring eyes.

If you can imagine loving yourself when you were a child, you can also love who you were when you were a teenager, or a young adult, and on and on. Accepting, forgiving, and celebrating who you are now will arise.

Yet, sometimes it is the feedback of significant others who light your way toward self knowing and amalgamation. If you wish to deepen the gift of integrity it often comes from other's you trust.

My Story in The Blue Veil: Curtains On Kirtan

"However veiled, the feminine is always naked" -Marion Woodman

The ego will tell you that you're not good enough no matter what you do. It always wants more validation since it fears death. It is longing to be loved and it can get quite hungry. You do need ego to develop a healthy self, yet in order to move to a higher spiritual development, you gently let it go. It is like releasing your childhood in order to attain adulthood.

> *"Inside everyone there is an emptiness that
> only God can fill-* Sri Daya Mata

As I urge women to express healthy egos in belly dancing, to overcome insecurities and inhibitions, I also remember that this means to use these powers wisely. Even after so many years I am still learning this for myself. When is the bliss of dance real and when is it not?

> *"The nature of the soul is power, bliss, love, eternal consciousness, omniscience, omnipresence. And so in all of the things man seeks in this world, he is trying to experience those qualities that are a part of his true nature. Analyze it; what is fame but the desire for immortality,*

*to be known while we're here, and to go on living in memory after
we're gone from this world. Man runs after these things because
he is unconsciously seeking to experience his own soul nature."*
- Sri Daya Mata, Self Realization Fellowship

Case in point! Recently, I attended a meditation conference in Los Angeles. The attendees had soulful eyes. Upon greeting on another, their kind nods bowed in reverence to each other's exquisite souls. The lectures concentrated on cosmic connection through meditation. Self-discipline, love, service, faith, and courage were all explored. Despite being a dancer who loves to move, I enjoyed the long meditations. Sometimes we sat for three hours or more. I meditate regularly, and have been doing so for many years. These assembled meditations, with so many people, were rich, full, and genuinely pleasing.

One early evening, after meditation, there was a Kirtan happening out on the lawn of the hotel. A group of musicians were gathered in a circle. Each played an exotic instrument such as a sitar, flute, cymbals or drums. Others were rocking, singing and chanting. To my belly dancing mind, it looked like a perfect invitation to dance. I took off my shoes, entered the circle and started belly dancing.

My friend who was attending the conference with me was not happy. She closed her eyes. I don't think she was praying! As a matter of fact, many people had their eyes closed. Yes others were smiling or using their phones to video me, but mostly, people were in their own reverie. What a strange audience. I only danced a few minutes, enjoying myself, and thanked the musicians for their beautiful music and went on with my day.

I've never encountered a meditating audience before. Was I dancing for them or for me? Was it an invitation, or did I invite myself? My dear friend thought it too sensual for the situation. I thought it was prayerful, but perhaps not to her. Was I inappropriate? Did they not want to see the body as spiritual? Could it be my boundaries were not sensitive enough? Was it so important for me to eagerly share my gifts, even if no one wanted or needed a gift at that time? Was it necessary for me to make myself the center of attention? What if no one knew I could dance like that, would it matter? Was I still loved and loveable without performing? And furthermore, how old was *that* thought? Or did I innocently want to share my joy? Probably both, since we are tricky beings.

If the ego was present in all its glory, it is still *"grist for the mill,"* as Ram Dass would say. How much was innocence, how much ego? Luckily there is such a thing as introspection...and also friendship.

My friend Bonnie, who invited me to join her on this path of meditation, has been my friend for over 20 years. I love her advice as she loves mine. We trust each other with our blind spots, with our full hearts, and yes even with our tricky minds. Many times we have brought each other to laughter, and I mean full belly laughs, with our own lack of insight. We highlight suppression that the other so skillfully unearths. She is the kind of friend who allows for a full measure of truth. She has been a catalyst for many changes in my life. She took me to my first yoga class before I became a yoga teacher. She invited me to her meditation group and the group lasted 15 years. Needless to say she is seemingly indispensible! So when she suggests something, I listen. Our sensibilities differ in many ways as she is more introverted, and I am more extraverted. We never cease to learn from one another, because of our differences, as well as in spite of them. If my dance seemed too sensual to her, maybe it was. And if it was not the best time and place for me to express myself, then restraint is just as important as self expression. Hmm...did I say that?

To top it all off, while having lunch with another dear friend Ellen, a psychologist, she suggested that perhaps my friend Bonnie had a point. Don't you just love that? It's the donkey's tail. An old adage that says "If three people call you a jackass, look to see if you have a tail." I wasn't about to ask another person!

> *"God gave us human relationships in various forms for one reason: we are to learn from one another. Everyone is in a sense our 'guru', our teacher...From all these relationships we acquire an expansion and purification of our love; and I believe that, in the ultimate sense, only love can change others. "*- Sri Daya Mata

Love of true friends can bring you to the sweet nectar of introspection, where you can gently face the uncomfortable with support. Pruning and restraint are just as important as progress and expression, in art, as well as in spiritual life. The gift of learning and self-correction goes on and on. Luckily, you don't have to do it alone.

Sisterhood and Belly Dancing

"Women who understand how powerful they are do not give into envy over meaningless things, instead they fight to maintain the beautiful bond of the sisterhood. These are the real women who know that we need each other's love and support to survive in this world. Love is the essence of being a woman. We must be that light of love that seals the bond and unique beauty of our sisterhood." –Bindu (famous Indian Actress)

I would be remiss if I did not mention sisterhood. It is one of the ways we learn integration; not only of the self, but also within a community. It is one of the mainstays of belly dancing. You assimilate with the women around you. It happens all the time, over and over again. Each group thinks it is totally unique and no one else could *possibly* be in a group like this. They could not *possibly* be given this great a gift. However, it is not unique. It is an absolute result of the dance!

It is often said that women live longer than men because they have each other. Married men live longer than single men because they have the company of a woman. Women are built for bonding. They carry children within, that they then care for. This insures the child's survival.

Sisters, full siblings, share approximately 50% of their genes as identical...100% for identical twin sisters. Yet beyond DNA, sisterly attachment thrives. I love my two brothers dearly. I learn so much from them in our trusted relationships. I learn about how men think, sometimes differently from women. I've mentioned how Russell valiantly stayed with me after a car accident, and my brother Warren, an otolaryngologist, actually saved my life when a fishbone was stuck in my throat. I remember trying to meditate in his office while he was removing the bone deeply embedded in my esophagus. It was tense. He was calling the hospital in case I needed a bed, but he was able to resolve the issue then and there. I trusted him implicitly. He has a great heart. The goodness of the beautiful men in my life is a treasured gift. My beloved son and husband also guide me in this area, as a deep place of solace, and soul connection. Yet sisterhood serves another place in tenderness.

When we were little, my true sister and I used to love to dress alike and pretend that we were twins. It was great fun to see how we looked like one another. As we grew, we would often try on clothing to let the other one know how she looked. We held hands at night to help us go to sleep. And although trickery, teasing and fighting happened, over the years it seems that few people got to know me better than my sister Pamela. I can say "You know what I mean," and she says "Hmm yes," and that can be the entire explanation. All those Hallmark cards become true when you trust your sister. Today my sister is an accomplished reading teacher. She teaches the little ones this arduous task with great patience and caring.

In gratitude for the deep abiding love I hold for my siblings, only my sister knows what it feels like to be a woman. The woman factor is unique. Having shared history as well as womanhood, we have an inimitable bond. Since my mother has passed away, I'm very grateful to have my sister's giving nature. It is the best reminder of the sweet mothering we shared, and have now lost.

When women belly dance together, similar connections materialize: sister-sharing, mother-daughter caring. Perhaps a triggered biological attachment happens. I've seen the phenomenon repeatedly as women belly dance their empathy and loyalty.

Belly dance allows a woman to cherish her feminine nature. She links herself to the Universe as a creative life-giving vessel of love. The dance is imbued with this knowledge. The body remembers. Feeling this alone would be daunting. Sharing it with sisters makes it real. For women, it requires overcoming eons of sexism, ageism, and oppression.

You evolve into full Goddess-hood. This takes spiritual courage, and so you reach out for the hand of a sister.

Sisters in sisterhood are thus: You think you are the only group like this! You acknowledge everyone's talent and beauty, even as you accept one another's frailties and faults. You have disagreements but work to heal them. The relationships continue to move from shallow to deep as the veils of separateness and self-consciousness fall away. Expectations and obligations become enjoyable devoted commitments. Rivalries and jealousies morph into sympathy and compassion. Instead of hierarchy and pecking order, connections form equality. Love is shared, and it grows. Through practice, performing, and costuming, you present yourself to the public. Sisterhood is received through dedication, risk, and loyalty. You become not only connected but interconnected. You take turns being strong and vulnerable.

Dr. Carol Gilligan, a pioneer in studying the development of girls, was a psychologist from Harvard who I have had the honor to meet. She is very dedicated to describing and exploring the feminine viewpoint. In her book *In a Different Voice*, She connotes adolescence as the moment when girls begin to doubt themselves. While 11-year-olds tend to be full of self-confidence, she said, by 15 and 16 they start to say, "I don't know, I don't know, I don't know." Some women stay at this stage. In sisterhood she can be channeled toward "knowing."

As a global community, we need to guard young girls against giving up on self development. We need to guide them toward their fullest evolvement as enlightened world beings. It is no small thing to share feeling, beliefs, and actions within sisterhood.

The challenge of answering to the call of sisterhood brings risk as well as support. Expectations can be unrealistic, favors exploited, and communications blurred. Selfishness and egoism can potentially ruin the happy family. If one sister is alienated, it is dangerous for her emotionally, and it is also felt by all. At times, the endurance skills of sisterhood appear more arduous than surviving a reality show! If care is not taken, the ancient risk of excommunication looms on the horizon. It is the ever unspoken threat. It has been said that women ostracize each other rather than fight…like men might. The sense of being left out begins with preadolescent girls. Is it the community way of keeping rules? Is it the feminine way of bullying? Perhaps it is an expression of not knowing how to properly find your voice and speak the truth. Women need caution not to sacrifice their own goals, integrity, or principles in this situation.

Gloria Steinem states in her book *The Revolution From Within,* that if we remain too comfortable in a group we cannot be growing. Some challenges must exist. How you handle them is of great importance to the overall development of women worldwide. As you practice conflict resolution, peace over being right, and compassion in the face of fear, bonds become strong and resilient. Over the years the sisterhood circle can become a safe haven within to rest your soul.

The moments shared with my belly dancing sisters have allowed the emerging swan of my childhood dreams to fly. As she flies with her flock, a rare and sacred image of beauty shines back from a still lake of friendship. The lake of sisterhood reflects the omniscient love of the Goddess.

Dancing and Aging

Group togetherness serves us eloquently, but some lessons of integration are even more personal. Some involve connecting with men. And eventually, as time goes by, you are even asked to integrate this love with aging! This can be quite a test! Dance and aging have similar challenges that echo this. I wrote this next poem when I was going through menopause. My husband was asking "What's going on with you?" and I answered "Nothing is going on with me…it's happening *to* me!"

My Thighs White

My thighs white
My body barren
My ass bigger
My breasts abundant for my small frame

My soul mourning fertile youth
My wisdom growing
My anger alive at some former version of myself,
for having abandoned me

I am woman now, at another stage
A ripened vine ready to fall
A flower curled at the edges
Fragrance changed
Death awaits one day
But much living is left

Union with me now and know secrets
Secrets prior unknown
This is no fertile place
This is no child unborn
But woman growing past childhood
Past motherhood
Past rules and into Nature

Unbridled and wandering to the unknown
Dare to journey with me?
Spiritual pursuits, ready or not
Want Mother Nature as your surrogate?
Symbiotic ride
My body is the guide, not me

Take the ride
I invite you like Eve and her apple
Closer to God and Goddess
Earthen roads, a blindfolded traveler
Have you the courage to be blind
Led by the blind?

I have no choice
I must follow
Perhaps you have a choice
The journey is mapped without my consent
Follow me if you will
Women are keepers of all the secrets

-MZN

After a time, the ease of aging began to change as acceptance grew. As I opened to compassion for myself, my perspective began to shift. So much suffering comes from not accepting things as they are. Why not be fully present for what is in the moment? Here is how the tone changed for me.

Aging into Softness
My skin is softer, but it still holds me
My legs are slower, yet they support my walk
My breath, not as deep, finds richness in appreciation
My mind, less black and white, practices compassion
My curves, much smoother now, are beautiful in proportion
Aging into softness, I come to know gentleness

-MZN

I'm older as I write this, and I have two performances next month. I'm sure the dance will go really well. After all I've had lots of practice. The questions become more about costuming. I do not have the skin of a twenty five year old, or the toned precise muscles I had at 30 or even 48. Being a grandmother is one of my greatest joys. Yet the aging process, for all of its wisdom and joy, leaves a dancer somewhat bereft. I hope that with a long beautiful wig and a push up bra, no one will know my age...if I dance fast enough!!

Where is it written that old people shouldn't dance? When I visited my 89 year old mother in her nursing home, entertainment was frequently provided. One afternoon, while a guitar player sang and enchanted the audience, a spry little old man, wearing an Irish hat, struggled out of his wheelchair. He wanted to stand and dance. His eyes and smile did more dancing than his thin, stiff body, yet all watching could feel the enthusiasm emanating from his shaky boogie. What is this impulse to move and celebrate?

You see a stark contrast between inner impulse and outer limitation. It's not popular to talk of these limitations. As Ram Dass once aptly expressed, "AARP would have us believe that old age and retirement bring new abilities for travel, golf, boating, tennis, dancing and more." Meanwhile the arthritis in my knees tell another story. A story of liberation from the body, a perspective of death. Can you dance about that? Of course, you can dance about anything!

For some, aging and sage-ing comes hard. You are too attached to your grace and beauty, and furthermore, you define yourself through those attributes. The release is challenging, humbling, yet also freeing. This vehicle of body can be overrated.

The nervousness of life, with all its exuberance, carries with it the adventure of overcoming obstacles. As you age, removal from hectic, frenetic energies emerges as a possibility. Your greatest work begins on another plane. The body begins to push you out. It is just not as comfortable or playful. The freedom you took for granted appears to have another agenda. So I dance because I can, knowing each fantastic flicker of the candle will ultimately burn out. I savor the flame.

Menopause and More

I am blessed to know Dr. Abigail Brenner. She is a psychiatrist and author, a dear friend and mentor. She has written many informative and fascinating books including *Replacement Child: The Unconscious Script*, a must read! It addresses what can happen to a child born after a previous child has died.

If not for her, I do not believe the book you are reading now would exist. While writing her book, *Women's Rites of Passage: How to Embrace Change and Celebrate Life*, she graciously included my story of passage and transition...as follows:

"Kismet II"

Kismet's Dance

Being a lifelong dancer, I did not take easily to the changes that "snuck up" on my body. When it came to the physical, I was accustomed to being in total control. But looking back from this vantage point, it seems that the threads that held my life together were being woven by a grander hand.

I used to imagine that someday my great-great-grandchildren would take a magical journey up the attic steps to a dusty old trunk, where they would find sparkling, shimmering, fascinating costumes, beads, and coins and veils, along with a very mystical, ancient photo of me—great-great-grandmother as Kismet. This would bring a smile to my lips, as I knew they would think, *"There was a life lived!"*

I have always loved to dance. As far back as I remember, the joy of 'being in my body' has always been with me. All I know of love and beauty, spirituality and God, has come from my body. It is this intimacy with Nature itself that I honor. It is this intimacy with the Divine spark within that has brought me glory and humility.

My parents encouraged my self-expression. I studied ballet, jazz, and even tap dancing. In high school, the budding student journalists captioned my yearbook photo, "Come Dance with Me." In a family of doctors, I became a teacher with a double master's degree in art and education, earning straight A's and a fellowship. Eventually, I taught fitness and dance.

I married young for love and had two children that both of us truly wanted. Natural childbirth and nursing deepened my soul's connection to my body as an instrument of Divine expression. I say that the universe borrowed my body to bring forth life. It was, at the time, the most spiritual event I had known.

Although my first husband was brilliant, sensitive, and charismatic; there were complex challenges in our marriage. We tried to hold it together, but that was not to be. Meanwhile, I found solace in becoming Kismet, the beloved one, through Oriental dance. Putting on Cleopatra-like makeup and adorning ancient costumes allowed me to become the veiled beauty who was one with the dance, one with feminine power and grace. I thought belly dancing was fantastically seductive, but what I really learned was that Mother Nature herself was the great seductress. This seduction was not about being a sex object or luring men; it was about the great power of the Feminine.

After twelve years of being a single parent, love came my way again. Only this time, my husband-to-be was brilliant, sensitive, charming, and filled with devotion. Over the years, my dancing transformed into fitness; my rich career expanded to include owning a fitness studio, where my daughter taught classes and my son worked the front desk and played drums for special workshops. I taught my students the "Sacred Wild Women Dance," a compilation of what I had learned about women and movement, even teaching instructors across the country and in Italy. I noticed the hunger in all women as I initiated their remembrance of the feminine legacy we all share.

Then this rite of passage snuck up on me. This one was different. I thought I had power and control—and then I couldn't sleep at night. Teaching fitness got harder; my whole system seemed to slow down. I spent one Mother's Day reading my children's baby books and crying that they would never be little again. My libido, my all-time connection to truth and life, was lessening. My breasts were becoming bigger and my shape more curvaceous. Who was I in this sauna of a hot flash? If I was not body beautiful, the sexy alluring lover, what was I? I saw images of flowering fallopians dying on the vine, once beautiful, now aging, once fertile, now self-contained. The *change* could not be happening to me! I talked, wrote poems, talked, meditated, cried, talked, published articles, danced, read, and talked until I was tired of listening to myself. If I took hormones, would I risk breast cancer? If not, would I die of a heart attack? I decided to stay the natural course.

One evening, my husband asked me what was going on. Why was I so different? All I could scream, through tears and shame, was *"I am not doing this. This is happening to me."* This menopause was a spiritually profound and heavy rite of passage, long and hard, an arduous process of learning to love and cultivate my inner soul, my loving kindness instead of the physical. Could I be loved for my essential self? It all comes together now. Using a yoga analogy, the love energy travels up from the sexual chakra into the heart chakra. I can now love more with my heart.

And what of these hot flashes? They are wake-up calls to herald the coming of the next great transformation: death. We lose youth and youth's beauty, and as we experience loss, we may also move toward losing inhibition, anger, and fear. This is a great letting go, not because we are so evolved, but because we have no choice but to surrender.

For me, to be a recipient of such great wisdom—to know secrets only women can know—is a precious thing. Women, the keepers of soulful connection, are called upon to notice soul beauty. We who know life within us must give birth to beauty and love. It is a deep primal rhythm of cycles and circles to experience with other women and to share with men. My body once again teaches spirit. This dance of menopause transcends, like all great art. It transcends the natural world, the nature of sex, not for procreation, fun, or even love of two, but sacred sex for the union of souls with the Divine---a practice of acceptance and compassion. Once again the universe borrowed my body to teach that it brings forth not only life, but love, a gentle and all-forgiving love, one that reminds me to honor my mother and father; to love my daughters and son and their spouses in a wiser and less possessive way; to share and learn from my husband, a great teacher of love himself; to dance with women celebrating our secret experiences of change; and to honor God in my every breath, my every breath until the last.

A peek into the future—up the attic stairs, into the dusty trunk—little hands open the creaky heavy lid, discovering treasures of their legacy. Did I tell you that in the ancient photo of Kismet, she is smiling? She sees the love and light in her great-great-grandchildren's eyes.

Integration and Mystery

How do you integrate the known and the unknown? Beyond integration of the self, beyond body and aging, you find your awareness drawn to other realms.

Once while meditating in a forest in Maine, I observed my mind's inclination to name things. I called one tree *baby tree*, another *sturdy*, another *verdant*, and so on. This distraction did not bring me deeper peace. The desire to name gives you a sense of ownership, even power. But it has a price. It differentiates a unified realm. You have learned to label and then to see accordingly.

"Paradox only exists in language"-John Daido Lorri, Zen Buddhist

Dance forces you to "un-lable" and therefore feel the encompassing universality of all things. You sense separation when using your mind to name and think. When you are speechless, you begin to sense a God who is frequently called the immutable, formless, unnamable mystery.

Baruch Hashem
Baruch Hashem in the name of the Father
The Son and the Holy Spirit
The blessed Mother
Lord Krishna
The Buddha
And Shakti and Shiva
And Protons and Neutrons and Quarks
And Black Holes and...
Let there be Light!
-MZN

Whatever we call "Integration," it is the melding of the self into "One." You can think, feel, and act with integrity. You can move toward that which is not harmful but helpful. You learn what contributes rather than what destroys. You see inclusion, not separateness. You glimpse that which is healed and whole. By cultivating a mindful-body and an embodied-mind, you can be fully alive.

Where does that lead? It leads to healing. It sheds light on your innate holiness. This escorts you toward a new connection. Do you see another Veil? Ah, shades of blue are turning toward another hue. What color is next? Where will it take you?

CHAPTER 6

THE PURPLE VEIL

The Sixth Veil: The Purple Veil of Promise

The purple veil is entrancing. Purple is uncommon in nature. If you go back to pre-historic existence, your ancestors rarely encountered a fruit, flower, or animal in purple. It is far more common now. Originally obtained from a dye, called murex, purple was extracted from a sea sail. This was a long and arduous process, which made acquiring it a rare gift. Yet, surprisingly, purple was one of the first colors used in prehistoric art. It was then made from ground rock pigments. It was used in the caves of France by Neolithic artists. Stranger still, purple, unlike violet, is not one of the colors of the rainbow. It is absent from the visible spectrum. You do see purple mountains majesty as an optical effect from the atmosphere. Because of all these qualities, purple tends to capture the imagination.

Due to this rarity, ancient people reserved it for royalty. In wavelengths of indigo, it has also stood for valor, as in the Purple Heart of bravery. Amethyst shades, during the woman's suffrage movement, symbolized women's right to vote. In Yoga chakras it denotes the third eye and inner wisdom.

Wrapped in the purple veil, you feel passion and self-discipline blend. You find freedom in devotion. Dancing within waves of purple veils, you promise to hold them close, and also, not to control them. A faithful partnership develops. Trust between you and the dance fosters intimacy. Flowing veils of violet, lavender and indigo combine the red of denial and desire, with the blue of integration and healing. Wrapped in the imperial colors bending toward fuchsia, you are regal and elegant. Like atmospheric changes you become lighter in your grasping. You promise to be present so the dance flows through you. You are the vessel of its cosmic intelligence. Growing lighter and lighter as you twirl, hazy shades of purple show you another vantage point.

Seven Wisdoms

- *Deepak Chopra, in The Seven Spiritual Laws of Success; the sixth law is the Law of Detachment:*

  > *The Law of Detachment, says that the way to acquire anything in the universe is to relinquish our attachment to it.. All we need to do is nurture our deepest intentions in our heart and go with the flow...surrender our desires to the creative mind that orchestrates the dance of the universe.*

  This implies that as you create, you let it go freely. Then, you reap the results. The inherent promise here, allows things to emerge. You promise to stay and remain open to uncertainty. In full faith, you stand your ground of commitment.

- *Yogi: Seven Stages of Development Before Achieving Complete Liberation*, in the sixth stage:
  The mind of the yogi becomes free of the influences of external natural processes whenever he desires so. Patanjali says:

  > *"Austerity, the study of sacred texts, and the dedication of action to God constitute the discipline of Mystic. Union...Liberation of the seer is the result of the disassociation of the seer and the seen, with the disappearance of ignorance."*

The "dedication" described here, is what I am calling the promise. It is devotion to practice in order to find freedom.

- Yoga Chakras: *the sixth Chakra is Anja:*

  Anja the "all knowing" third eye chakra: Above the nose and between eyebrows lies the Third Eye...Intuition—The right to "see." (beyond).
  Trusting one's intuition and insights. Developing one's psychic abilities.
  Self-realization. Releasing hidden and repressed negative thoughts.
  It is at this point that the two side nadis Ida and Pingala are said to terminate and merge with the central channel Sushumna, signifying the end of duality.
  (e.g. light and dark, or male and female).

Here is another way of knowing, outside of logic. It is the bridge to deeper understandings. The promise to bridge intuition with performance is peak. It uses the third eye as guidance.

- *Kohlberg's Stages of Moral Development : Stage* 6:

  The morality of conscience: An orientation, not only toward existing social rules, but also toward the conscience as a directing agent, including mutual trust and respect, and principles of moral choice involving logical universalities and consistency.
  Action is controlled by internalized ideals that exert a pressure to act accordingly regardless of the reactions of others in the immediate environment. If one acts otherwise, self-condemnation and guilt result.

In psychological terms the super-conscience guides you toward a more mindful way of living. It is the promise of acting on what you perceive to be most moral.

- *Dr. Clarissa Pinkola Estes discusses the sixth stage of love as:*

   Heart as Drum and Singing Up:

   The story contains this promise: allow Skeleton woman to become more palpable in your life, and she will make your life larger in return.

Skeleton woman represents the skeletons in your closet. Also, the ones in your psyche—your hidden shadowed darkness. *Skeleton woman* signifies that which is bare and needs to be fleshed out. Committing to investigating this process is a promise. Your ability to accept the not-beautiful and to love it with compassion, is to stay the course of love.

- *Buddhism, the Seven Factors of Enlightenment, the sixth factor is:*

   Concentration, samadhi, a calm, one-pointed state of concentration of mind.

In Buddhism, this stage is considered a precursor to enlightenment. At this level of consciousness, the mind is in one-pointed concentration. The person remains conscious of this. Upon development of *samadhi,* one's mind is said to become temporarily purified of defilements. It is calm, tranquil, and luminous. There are various kinds of Samadhi. Once the meditator achieves a strong and powerful concentration, his or her mind is ready to penetrate the ultimate nature of reality. Eventually release from all suffering arrives. The final stage would be reached by the next veil.

- ***The Sixth Mystical Secret of the Veils: The Purple Veil of Promise:***

Promise Unveils Divine Connection

"Michelangelo"

In the purple veil you learn to promise. As you commit, happy coincidences arrive. They guide you toward Divine connection. You see your Self as a God-realized being.

Experiential Dance Activities:

- ○ *Beautiful Face, Beautiful Body, Beautiful Soul Dance:* As you belly dance, hover over your face, body, and heart, with your hands gracefully. As if you are speaking with your hands say: "I have a beautiful face, I have a beautiful body, my soul is full of beauty." Can you experience yourself as beautiful and promise to honor that?
- ○ *Dance to God:* Open your entire being to the Divine Source.
- ○ *Practice a Routine*: practice until you think it is as perfect as you can make it!

- o *Welcoming or Rejecting Dance*: Face a partner and then express acceptance or rejection. Notice how it feels to accept or reject others.
- o *Archetype Dance*: Dance and be the warrior woman, wild woman, goddess woman: Try on different aspects of yourself. See how strong or weak the impulses are that guide you. What do you intuit?

Promise and Imagination

Life is an interactive process. Like all creative endeavors, it requires imagination. Imagination connects you to the very nature of art. Vast cultural memories are within you. Noting exists in isolation. Not even you. You are part of the cosmic masterpiece of life. Once you promise to acknowledge this, you can relax and move out of the way. Inspiration invites itself in. It shows you connection. You not only dance now, you create dance, and it creates you. Then you are gone, and then there is nothing but creation.

"Of course, stories have a way of emerging out of nowhere. Rather than making them up, we seem, instead, to find them; it may even be more accurate to say they find us."- unknown

With Promise, you have cultured a commitment to higher consciousness, even in action. You want to *be* the Ten-Commandments, the Four Noble Truths, the Sanatana Dharma, the Pillars of Islam and the Classics of Confucianism, not just follow them. You want to *be* them, and thereby connect with higher knowing. Think of the Ten Commandments as a description rather than a list of rules. If you are one who honors God and your parents, and you avoid killing, adultery, stealing, coveting, and lying, what sort of person are you then? You would have made a pledge to remain aware. You would use your wisdom in devotion to whatever arises. You would stay with "what is." Now, accept the promise. It connects you to a Divine realm.

Psychic guidance visits you. You become aware of the freedom in self-discipline. You address intuition as internal knowing. You perform with trust as an expression of faith. Doubt still exists. Yet you have set creativity free precisely because you promised. You promised to remain even when in doubt.

You are dancing with the purple veil. Even though you falter and fail, you remain steadfast. The dance arises magically when you remain present. So you stay. You are captivated by the invisible becoming visible. You are entrusted to the process. This commitment to a higher promise changes everything for the better. You are entering the promise-performance level. The universe wants to support you. This vow has power.

Perfection and Promise

> *"The yearning for our lost perfection, the urge to do and be that which is the noblest, the most beautiful of which we are capable, is the creative impulse of every high achievement. We strive for perfection here because we long to be restored to our oneness with God.* -Paramahansa Yogananda

April Rose Dancer, a world class belly dancer, who has been a principal performer with Miles Copeland's groundbreaking commercial dance company Bellydance Superstars, offers this eloquent quote about perfection:

> *"Here is the big secret: the ideal is unattainable. The perfection we are moving toward, through disciplined practice, will never be reached. Our artworks will never be the fullest expression of themselves. Knowing this, we continue the journey anyway. The unending journey is one of the most valuable and essentially human things we can do. Enjoy the ride."*

In creating any art you are striving toward perfection. Yet you don't have to be perfect. Only God is perfect. It is the striving that is essential. If you are preoccupied with being perfect you get in your own way. It is through seeing your imperfections that you change and grow. It is from your mistakes that you learn.

When you give a performance you have intention. When you promise to do your best, the communion between you and the Divine appears. It has to do with transformation of energy: thought-vibration, movement through space, and other hidden forces at play. It is significant for a dancer that the energy she feels is transmitted to the audience. That force goes through the audience. In dance, no words have been spoken, all is in the vigor of physical and soulful expression. The message is visual yet tactile. This connects you to primitive, pre-verbal, instinctual knowing. The energy of the dance ripples out to the audience. Not just the audience of matter, but also the audience of thought-vibration and shared emotion. This ripple effect reminds me of what happened a few days ago…or should I say daze?

My Story in the Purple Veil: Crazy Daze Vortex

We all have days like this. I went out of the house to empty the garbage, sans shoes, sox, and phone, only to find that I was now locked out! Luckily I was able to climb over the balcony and find the welcoming back door open. Later, I tried to start my car but the battery failed. Luckily the AAA repair man started it for me. I tipped him my last several dollars. A little stressed from my "ordeals," I decided to take the ten minute drive across the Atlantic Beach Bridge, to meditate by the ocean. When I arrived at the bridge, I had no cash, after tipping the nice repair man. And, my pass for the bridge had expired. The toll booth woman suggested I pull over and buy a new pass. Handing the bridge authority receptionist my credit card, he informed me that his computer was down. He would accept cash, which of course I did not have. If I had, I would have been over the bridge by now, but I didn't tell him that. Instead I fumbled in my purse and luckily found an old crumpled check. I then wrote out an amount for the entire seasonal pass to cross over the bridge. A good choice. Presumably I would go to the sea and meditate many times now.

Finally, I arrived on the beach for meditation. Ah, the water was so calm I wondered at it being the Atlantic. The sand was warm and welcoming. I absentmindedly drew hearts and decorated them with the small black muscle shells strewn about. Satisfied with my state of mind, and my artwork, I meandered back to the car. There it was, as I had left it, only now a huge white truck was parked behind it, blocking my path. Three robust people were unloading some sort of boxed wood. I asked if they could please move the truck so I could back out. They replied that they were too busy unloading. With practiced patience, I luckily saw one friendly working woman offer to guide me and my car out through a narrow passage to freedom.

Feeling valiant at overcoming problems by now, I once again crossed over the bridge. All was going well. Later that afternoon, after meeting with my "Diva" friends to assist with their rehearsal, I fell flat on my butt while trying to say a graceful goodbye! Luckily, I was more humiliated than hurt.

These events remind me of the famous story about a Chinese frontiersman and farmer. The story dates back to 139 B.C., and it is said to have come from nomadic people who lived near the region of Xiongnu. The story has a Zen like quality, and it goes like this:

One day a poor farmer and his son bought a horse to help work the farm. The next day the horse ran away. Neighbors said, "What bad luck." The farmer replied, "Maybe yes, maybe no." The horse returned the next day with a wild stallion. Neighbors said, "What good luck!" The farmer replied, "Maybe yes, maybe no." The farmer's son tried to break the stallion, only to fall and break his own leg. Neighbors said, "What bad luck." The farmer replied, "Maybe yes, maybe no." Having a broken leg then prevented the son from being inducted into the army. Neighbors said, "What good luck!" The farmer replied, "Maybe yes, maybe no."...and the story goes on and on in a never ending cycle.

Life is like that. Predicaments of up and down, obstacle and resolution, and blockades versus freedom occur in successive and repetitive patterns. Whether or not the outcome is good or bad remains to be seen over time. Yet when unlikely occurrences happen with similar patterns, we wonder at the quality of chance. Do they imply intention? Is it all random? Did I co-create this energy? What energy was I in anyway? Where did it come from? Truth be told, I was not in a good space. I had been worried about a sick relative on the pinnacle of life and death. Throw in a few concerns about the grandchildren and children, and that was my state of mind. Worry! Worry can be a sticky spiritual challenge.

But can worry alter your reality? Perhaps it is like the ripple influence of the dancer and the audience. Could matter and space-time mirror the quality of experience? Maybe I could alter my alignment through further meditation, dance, or prayer. I think I'm about to use that bridge pass for another mini-meditation. After all, if the world is my audience, I'd dearly love to intend a most graceful dance.

Part of the promise-performance level, then, is to use all the learning of the previous veils. All the skillful tools get tested from time to time. It is definitely not only an uphill climb. As stated, these guidelines are only a template. Each of you have your own distinct path to honor and hone. Respect your process and promise to stay on the path. See what you find. We are all journeying it together. Let your imagination help.

Imagination Required

"I am enough of an artist to draw freely upon my imagination. Imagination is more important than knowledge."- Albert Einstein

Imagination requires promise. Watch a child at play. Children are hard-working at play. Remember the intense concentration you had as a child? Imagination was required. Make-believe captured all of your attention. You promised not to break the spell! In adulthood, this is called the arts. And it requires commitment.

When belly dancing, your entire being is present at this *work* of Art. With the intensity of child-play, a visceral knowing mixes with imagination. There is no mistaking its meaning. The DNA memory existing within you wants to be known. Your body remembers. You become the work of art.

As a woman practices belly dance she "tries on" different aspects of the feminine. By play-acting the Goddess, she stirs her inner life into being. It is as if her dreams come true. Jungian analyst and author Jean Shinoda Bolen, M.D. states:

> *"Women...drawn to a particular mythological goddess found that this archetype affected their dreaming life or waking imagination. Goddesses sometimes appeared in these dreams as numinous or awesome and mysterious figures. ...figures and mythic themes that reside deep in the collective unconscious merged into consciousness."*

In contrast, some scientists assert that imagination is counterfactual. That it is an alternative to reality, or even an avoidance. It is seen as an outgrowth of problem-solving, asking questions like "What if?" or "How else could I do this?" Or "What could happen when this happens?" Is imagination merely a survival skill? Does that explain art?

Art is the playground of imagination. Applying make-up and wearing Cleopatra's costume, evokes images of little girls playing dress-up. Remember when you pretended that you were all grown up? You can see the value of that. What happens when an adult does it? Costuming becomes a designing of identity.

Picture a mother, doctor, lawyer, police-woman, or secretary, applying exotic eye make-up. See her dressing in a coined bra, beaded hip belt, and sequined veils. Using physicality for a shift in spirit, in this conversion she grants herself permission to awaken the Goddess. The mysterious-one that guides her, the knowing-one who leads her to intuition, the loving-one who sees only her beauty, and the terrible-one who reminds her of her time of death. In her promise she senses all these connections.

Dance and Grace

Costumed or not, you may dance alone in your room, on a beach, or in a studio. You dance with a partner, with your tribe, or you dance to God. The joy comes with or without an audience. Who do you dance for? What is the meaning of your dance? Dancing at the promise mastery level invites mysteries to reveal themselves. Ancient secrets are teaching *you* now. They are coming because you *promised* to receive them.

I can see them. I marvel at the different kinds of physical expression people have. Yes, I may be teaching the same dance, but somehow each person holds an exclusive formula. Your life is reflected in your rhythmic gyrations. I can intuit if you were touched kindly, if you were rocked as a child, if your boundaries were respected. I know if you are comfortable with self expression, if you twist away, hunch over, aggress or use different spacing between yourself and others. I can feel whether or not you think you are beautiful. I witness where you hold tension, and where you release. You all see and sense this too, perhaps on a subconscious level. It is what creates exceptional irreplaceable art, that "one of a kind" dance-canvas where your body expression is unique. It also holds a place in the healing realm. Your body may reveal things which can be brought to the light.

Just as water takes the form of that which holds it, a dancer can yield to loveliness. Agility requires being strong and relaxed simultaneously. Belly dance, in particular, requires shaking and snaking. It is a practice of congruently relaxing and tensing muscles. The shaking creates shimmies. The snaking creates undulations.

Suppleness that savors the moment cannot be rushed. You stay to finish a gesture down to the last stretch of the fingertips, the tilt of the head, and the focus of the eye. There is deference for the in-breath, the out-breath, and the space in-between. This means you stand in your promise to remain open to immeasurable beauty, and you let it pass through you. Grace is fed by a sense of deservability. It comes when you receive it.

When you see a graceful dancer she is moving like nature...naturally. It calls to mind a cat stalking, a cloud passing, zigzag lightening linking heaven and earth, or perchance, the gentle caress of a mother cradling her baby. Grace invites inter-being. There exists a faith that the dancer will not fall or be awkward. Surrender has begun. Gratefulness awakens. You have been given gifts, and you promise to share them. Inherent in the promise you become aware of communion.

"If you are gifted artistic talents, you are morally obligated to share those gifts." -Deborah Luken: Artist

When offering gifts, you get past self-judgment. If you desire transformation, then *dance like no one is watching*—not even yourself. The promise steps in and delivers your true gifts. One dancer I worked with did just that:

Grace M.I.A.

I offer one-on-one sessions for semi-pro and professional belly dancers. It's like putting make-up on an already beautiful face. However, many years ago I had a dancer come to me who challenged that delight. She had an awkward, jarring way of dancing. Her moves were antithetical to belly dancing. What was I to do? She was eager, fit, and adoring the dance. Frankly, I could not imagine her learning it. She purchased costumes, began to sew her own with great aptitude, and came faithfully for lessons. Determined to get a professional dance job, she attended the most favorable performances to watch and learn. What puzzled me was that she could learn choreography, steps, rhythms, finger cymbals, and more...yet some indefinable grace was M.I.A.

I cared for her, respected her sewing talents, bought costumes from her, practiced teaching her with patience, and finally grew to love her. Then, surprisingly I became *her* student! She taught me an important lesson. *Never underestimate what someone can learn.* Especially if they make the promise!

Over time, she turned out to be alluringly graceful. She flourished as a successful professional dancer. Her beautifully designed costumes were well-sought-out by fellow dancers. I know now, that paying close attention helps someone move toward grace. Her promise inspired mine. A shared promise increases the power.

There is a sub plot to this dancer's story. Her boyfriend, who accompanied her to each and every lesson, told me a curious narrative. I noticed, as he spoke, that *he* was tall, strong, considerably older, and markedly graceful as he moved and talked. He shared a strange tale. For years he worked at a delicatessen, carrying heavy boxes up and down a long flight of stairs. One day he fell and became instantly paralyzed... totally paralyzed! He could not move a muscle for seven years.

A long burdensome endurance ensued. He suffered physically. In addition, not knowing his fate was the strangest difficulty of all. In spite of that, he did not give up on the idea of healing. You could say he promised to keep the faith! One day, during physical therapy, while being bathed, he saw his big toe move. Miraculously, that small but momentous event marked the beginning of his complete restoration.

As I write this, I am aware of the foreshadowing his story held. It mirrored my forthcoming broken back. It illustrated the healing process I too would endure. Perhaps having heard his story, and having it in my unconscious memory, gave me extra courage. Like a secret pledge, it helped me regain my own grace.

Muscle has memory. The body is consciousness expressed in matter. All manner of impressions can be made upon the psyche and the body. They become embodied as defensive blocks to freedom or invitations to heal. Many children are not handled with the gentleness that might offer them natural poise. With time that can be healed. Let us give praise to parents that remember to be kind, touching their children with gentleness and love. Perhaps they create graceful dancers.

The beautiful elegance of a dancer reminds you that a gentle bearing can be brought to every level of life. When you handle everyday responsibilities, do you rush, push things around, reach for things in a crude manner? Or do you take time to do your work gracefully? The way you feel about everyday obligations can be altered by adding a sense of ease to the task.

"Walk as if you are kissing the Earth with your feet."- Thich Nhat Hanh, *Peace is Every Step: The Path of Mindfulness in Everyday Life*

There is also an expanded definition of *grace*, as in the expression, "*by the grace of God.*" Divine guidance is then giving you the "OK" sign. You are going in the right direction. Synchronicity, a term coined by the famous psychologist Carl Gustav Jung, is defined as "a meaningful coincidence; two juxtaposed experiences surprisingly related." Here is a simple example.

I was putting my granddaughter Quinn to bed and reading her a story. She wanted to read the book *The Original Mother Goose*. I had written an inscription on the inside cover which read "I await your arrival…Love, Nanny." I told her I bought the book before she was born. She smiled. It was a sweet moment. Later, on the drive home I was listening to a classical station, and an enchanting piece of music came on. It was so charming that I was eager to hear the announcer tell me what it was. He said "That was the score of Mother Goose". Hmm.

Look for synchronicities and write them down. They are signs that your journey is heading in the right direction. As Deepak Chopra says in his book *Synchrodestiny: Harnessing the Infinite Power of Coincidence to Create Miracles*:

"According to Vedanta, there are only two symptoms of enlightenment, just two indications that a transformation is taking place within you toward a higher consciousness. The first symptom is that you stop worrying. Things don't bother you anymore. You become light-hearted and full of joy. The second symptom is that you encounter more and more meaningful coincidences in your life, more and more synchronicities. And this accelerates to the point where you actually experience the miraculous."

Sprit moves into matter and you move matter back to spirit. Especially as you become a devoted dancer in the dance of life. As you trust, your promise is fulfilled.

My Teacher Dahlena

As stated earlier, my encounter with belly dancing came to me as a synchronicity. I was living in a place that had a clubhouse, and belly dancers came to teach, just at the time I was yearning for a dance class. After several teachers of Middle Eastern Dance, I was guided toward Dahlena.

Dahlena was my most influential instructor in the dance world. All of my teachers contributed their best, yet Dahlena's mastery inspired me to love and commit to Middle Eastern Dance. It became my vow, and she helped me define it.

My strict ballet teacher "encouraged" me to take classes with 6 year olds when I was sixteen, presumably to help me review and catch up. I was humiliated, and eager to learn quickly, just to get out of the baby class! My jazz teacher requested that I perform at the New York World's Fair, and at Opera Showcases. She shared invaluable information about perfume, grinding ballet shoes into resin, and scoring the bottom of my jazz shoes. A large safety pin was used prior to pouring Coke on the bottom of the shoes in order to make them sticky. This helped us avoid tripping. When another teacher shunned air conditioning during sweltering summer days, the summer sweat at the dance bar increased my flexibility by twice, it seemed. Each teacher gave whatever gifts she had to inspire me. They made a huge difference in my life. All the small gestures may have been underestimated at the time, but something kept me wanting to learn more. Now I know. When someone sincerely takes an interest in your progress, you become better and better under their loving guidance. They made an unspoken promise!

Dahlena was such a teacher. She always did her best, so I was encouraged to do mine. Her dedication to artistry was contagious. She lead the dance troupe with love, patience, and persistence. It is no surprise that her artful choreography lofted belly dancing to new heights. It became a legitimate art-form, and a celebrated balance of culture and beauty under her tutelage, because of her dedication as much as her talent. She is modest, yet her fame elevated and spread this precious dance. She kept it alive. She is still teaching and dancing. Here is her contribution to this book.

"Dahlena, My Teacher"

A Short Description of Dance and What it Means to Me
by Dahlena

Dance has been a very important part of my life. Without giving details, I had a tumultuous childhood; dance became an escape for me. In my early years I had no formal dance training, I would try to copy the dance moves from the movies. I also made costumes from crepe paper and Christmas tree trimmings.

In Junior high we had tumbling, now called gymnastics, so I became flexible and strong. We performed at half time for some of the basketball games. I loved it, but at home I would still play music and just improvise some kind of dance.

A few years later when I moved to the big City, I started ballet. Jump ahead a couple of years to Boston. In Boston I was performing in a Night Club Chorus line, and the featured dancer was a Belly

161

Dancer. The moves and the music were so attractive. I felt a strong connection, and wanted to learn more. That year I did become an "Oriental Dancer." That is the title that was used in those days. It was wonderful – something I could do Solo, and also express the music with more emotion, and be transformed to a place of joy.

A few more years down the road of my Dance journey, I left the Night Clubs and stared teaching. The Dance has taken me on a journey I would never have thought possible, most came to me as opportunities to explore more areas of Middle East Dance and Music. Taking the dance out of the Night Club to the Concert stage with regional dances and costumes was expanding my view and appreciation of Dance. Creating Choreography and designing costumes for our dance company was so inspiring. This process drew something out of me. I will always wonder how I did all of this: watching how wonderful it is to see dancers performing, with beautiful costumes, on stage, to your creation is a magical experience. I had a lot of support from my dancers and friends that helped to make this happen. Dance brings people together in ways it is difficult to put into words.

The dance not only took me on a journey across the U.S. - also to Foreign Countries that at one time I could only dream of. On the plus side I could make money doing something I loved and along the way have made many wonderful friends.

I have experienced the support and kindness of many people that have helped to make this journey a wonderful experience. I would especially like to thank my dear friends Jane Coles and Yousef Moshe who are sadly no longer with us. Their friendship and support was a big part of my life for a few years.

As one person expressed to me about my dance history, "You, Dahlena, have had a blessed career." Yes, I feel very fortunate to have worked with so many talented people. Although there have been a few pebbles in my path, I can say I have been very fortunate and there are many people to thank along the way for my success.

It is important not to get stuck, I try to keep up with the flow but, only use music and movement that I can connect to and can be transformed to a joyous place, sometimes a magical place. It is important to keep my body strong and somewhat flexible to be able to express the music freely through body movement...To feel free --There is no freedom without discipline. Don't know who said this, but it is so true.

Wisdom and Promise

Perhaps Dahlena's discipline is a kind of promise. This promise relates to wisdom. At one time it was important to acknowledge my gift of dance. It was only later that I learned these gifts are Divine, not mine. Wisdom is your divine gift as well.

The continuum from ignorance to knowing is a spiritual quest. There is a theme threading through your life. If you but look back, you will see it. The story of your life is the story of your soul. A promise, or pledge, to be your authentic self, means to follow your true quest.

Eventually wisdom becomes a practice of discerning your truth. This can get risky. My mother used to say "There are three sides to any story: his story, her story, and the truth." Memory is tricky. People don't concur on what they recall. Experiences are filtered through wants and expectations. Although this can be used to your advantage when using imagination, it doesn't work very well when reviewing a crime scene.

If you commit to wisdom and remain open, then experience becomes a great teacher. You learn from your mistakes, your misfortune, and your success. As you practice discernment perspective widens. Choices come from a place of promising to do your best at being wise.

To be wise implies that you see connection, not separateness. To be wise you distinguish good from bad choices, and make those choices through love. To be wise you are able to keep learning. Not to be stagnant and stuck, but organically flowing with "what is," while remaining open to ever increasing awareness. It means navigating the uncomfortable to find release. As Oprah Winfey says: "Turn your wounds into wisdom."

Some wisdom teachings come harder than others. It helps to remember that you are not alone. Wisdom may mean getting feedback from trusted others, and of course it means checking in with the self...

over and over again. Remain open in the heart, not just the head, and illuminations will arise. Anyone who has experienced an altered state of consciousness can attest to love being more real than reality.

To be wise is to do the *dance* of wisdom. Like any other dance, that means remain pliant, stretch beyond your usual limits, and change pace as needed. Seek harmony, beauty, and truth with a natural rhythm without force. Stay awake as you surrender. This will lead you to the next veil. See it just ahead....it is calling you to the next dimension.

CHAPTER 7

THE WHITE VEIL

The Seventh Veil: The White Veil of Stillness

"You do not need to leave your room. Remain sitting at your table and listen. Do not even listen, simply wait, be quiet, still and solitary. The world will freely offer itself to you to be unmasked, it has no choice, it will roll in ecstasy at your feet." — Franz Kafka

You may have your own unique approach for this veil. Call it *spirit*, *bliss*, or *surrender*. Perhaps *spaciousness* or *equanimity* might be better. Maybe *allowing*, or *relinquishing* would serve to explain it. Would *acceptance* suffice? It specializes in being vague!

Yet you yield and stay. As you release the white veil, you watch it ripple and take form. You let it go. You watch its configuration. Then in has none. You have set free your spoken word, your dance gesture, your elemental self-expression. Where does this expression come from, where does it go? You do nothing to know nothing. You do nothing to know everything. Be calm and tranquil, as you celebrate the Sabbath, and give up all struggle. You lose yourself and merge with what is, to know peace.

Oh the Dance
By Davira Bareli

Oh the dance,
How the breath moves me as it reaches the depth of my being,
Spirit comes thru me,
My hips sway from side to side, up and down and round and round.
My body begins to undulate as it weaves
thru the past, present and future
And the real "I" awakens.
My energy illuminates and sparks a fire deep within.
I am no longer bound by time or space.
Reality as I know it no longer exists.
The false pretense has fallen away;
True reality fills every crevice of my sensing self.
My consciousness has expanded,
I am connected to all that is, was, and will be.
I have transformed from the physical into an eternal spark of divinity
As I effortlessly express my whole being.
I spin, turn and whirl like an all knowing angel.
My body yearns to open as my soul confirms
that I am even greater than I can ever possibly imagine.
Pure bliss, complete and total freedom on all levels of existence.
I dance, I breathe, I move, I am alive like never before.
Oh the dance...

Davira is dancing in the white veil. As you dance with this veil, it fades into oblivion. As sheerness evaporates, it becomes nothing; the nothing from which all existence arises. And so the veil disappears and reappears. You may associate white with soft billowy clouds, or a blanket of snow. Perhaps sweet warm milk, ice crystals on trees, peace-doves, or starlight in an ebony sky.

Materials that do not emit light, appear white. White is an achromatic color, literally a color without color. It is composed of all frequencies of the visible spectrum. Objects appear white because they reflect all colors. The object does not absorb any wavelength. All the light is scattered to your eyes. White is dazzling. Thought of as no color, white holds ethereal qualities of the mysterious. When the white veil swirls around you, it is as if *you* appear and disappear. Perhaps you are doing just that. You are dancing within the mystical.

The Gifts of the River

There was a time I was entranced by my own dazzling image—my belly dancing self. It was part of my needed journey toward self-love. I was enthralled by my gift of dance, and how beautiful I could become. I moved in and out of this image. Where was my true self in this image? A smaller less confident me was searching for strength. Underneath the layers of silk and shiny jewels was a woman trying to prove that she too had value.

I did hold a secret intuition that the dancer I personified held some strange intrinsic beauty. After I discovered "her," that created a new dilemma. Could she appear and then disappear at will? Was that her when she was in costume, or when she was not in costume? Subsequently, I have spent the first half of my life learning to love myself, and the second half learning to relinquish the self! This happens in the white veil. You and the self, and the no-self merge. All the while dancing in a creative flow with the alluring river of light, Divine light.

While dancing in the white veil, it is important to acknowledge these gifts; they are Divine, not mine. You become a vessel in the spiritual quest. You receive the gifts. If you but look back, you will see how the drop of water became the river. You are part of a vast legacy. You contribute to an ever-changing stream. Sometimes you make momentum, sometimes you are carried, and sometimes you surrender. Faith grows in this relinquishing surrender. It is noticing that the river will hold you while you float.

"Let us imagine that life is a river. Most people are clinging to the bank, afraid to let go and risk being carried along by the current of the river. At a certain point, each person must be willing to simply let go, and trust the river to carry him or her along safely. At this point he learns to "go with the flow" and it feels wonderful.

Once he has gotten used to being in the flow of the river, he can begin to look ahead and guide his own course onward, deciding where the course looks best, steering his way around boulders and snags, and choosing which of the many channels and branches of the river he prefers to follow, all the while, still "going with the flow."
　　　　　　　　　- Shakti Gawain, *Creative Visualization*

Seven Wisdoms

*　•　Deepak Chopra, in The Seven Spiritual Laws of Success, the seventh law is:*

The Law of Dharma...Use your gifts and talents to serve.

　　When you use your gifts and talents to serve, you allow the creative flow to use you. It is not by you, or of you, but through you. This reminds me of the quote from Kahlil Gibran in his book *The Prophet* about children:

"Your children are not your children. They are the sons and daughters of Life's longing for itself. They come through you but not from you, and though they are with you yet they belong not to you. You may give them your love but not your thoughts, for they have their own thoughts. You may house their bodies but not their souls, for their souls dwell in the house of tomorrow,..."

　　Creativity is also the child born of you. It is not for keeping, but for sharing.

- *Yogi: Seven Stages of Development Before Achieving Complete Liberation, in the seventh stage:*

   The Self of the yogi becomes identical with Pursha and the state of absolute freedom, Kaivalya, is achieved.

   This "freedom" comes from surrender of the self into a greater knowing than you are capable of on your own. It is the story writing you, the canvas painting itself, and the dance dancing you.

- *Yoga Chakras: the seventh Chakra is Sahasrara"*

   Sahasrara, "thousand spokes: "crown-chakra"
   ...crown of the head...knowingness...the right to aspire
   ...dedication to the divine consciousness
   and trusting the universe.

   Your connection to the concept of "God," or a higher intelligence happens here. Your consciousness and subconsciousness evolve into superconsciousness. Sahasrara's inner aspect deals with the release of karma. It combines physical action with meditation, mental action with universal consciousness, and emotional action with "beingness."

- *Kohlberg's Stages of Moral Development : Stage 7:*

   Kohlberg suggested that there may be a
   seventh stage — Transcendental Morality,
   or Morality of Cosmic Orientation — which
   linked religion with moral reasoning.

   Ordinary moral reasoning must become extraordinary when it moves into the seventh stage. Here faith takes a part in reasoning. Kohlberg points to *agape* as a form of stage seven. *Agape* in Greek means the love that is, of, and from God, whose very nature is love itself.

"Whoever does not love does not know God,
because God is love."- John 4:8

This love is distinguished from erotic love. Agape can mean a-gape...wide open, as a mouth in awe.

'Agape' is an ethic that presupposes justice principles
but goes beyond them. He (Kohlberg) describes it
as 'an ethic of responsible universal love, service, or
sacrifice -an ethic of supererogation'.-Some Thoughts
on Kohlberg's 'Stage 7 -by Anne Garvey, Ph.D

• Dr. Clarissa Pinkola Estes discusses the seventh stage of love as:

"The Dance of Body and Soul."

"Through their bodies, women live very close
to the Life/Death/Life nature.
When women are in their right instinctual minds, their ideas
and impulse to love, to create, to believe, to desire are born,
have their time, fade and die, and are reborn again."
"Yet love in its fullest form is a series of deaths and rebirths."

This Life/Death/Life cycle is surely one of creativity and receptivity. And what greater surrender is there than death? You relinquish. You surrender to life, to love, and finally to God.

• *Buddhism, the Seven Factors of Enlightenment, the seventh factor is:*

Equanimity upekkha: to be fully aware of all
phenomena without being lustful or averse
towards them (free in the awareness).

Serene neutrality enables an equanimity that sees all beings impartially. Here you surrender to "what is," which cultivates peace of mind.

- *The Seventh Mystical Secret of the Veils: The White Veil of Stillness:*

Stillness Unveils Peace

In the white veil you surrender. Not as a *giving up* of freedom, but as a pathway to freedom. Paradox prevails. This offering of Self to the Divine actually expands you. You join with all that is, into a merging consciousness...being with the *One*.

Experiential Dance Activities:

- ○ *Loud to Quiet Dance*: Dance for awhile to loud music until you are out of breath, and then sit still, and stay still, until peace envelopes you. What is the contrast between full and empty...loud and quiet...busy and calm....what energy do you experience?
- ○ *Sustained Dance*: Dance long sustained movements slowly and without stopping. If you align with the energy that is slow and sustained you begin to experience the feeling of effortless energy.
- ○ *Share the Energy Dance*: Sit in a circle of people, and dance passing invisible energy around the circle, as if passing a ball of luminous light. Can you share the energy of who you are in an easy way...where there is no force, only peace?
- ○ *Guided Dance*: Close the circle around one person. As they dance in the center everyone guides them by touching them physically and gently as they close their eyes. Can you feel the support of the universe as you are guided by others?
- ○ *Puppet Dance*: One person hangs as a puppet, and the other, "Giapetta," puts the "puppet" body into a belly dance position. When finished, switch roles. When your body lets go, how does your mind react? Can you really let yourself be guided?
- ○ *Veil Throw*: Throw your veil up in the air, and see how it lands... do this a few times: notice how it is different each time...see

how everything unveils...how you are part of a great unveiling of truth and love that has a subtle force which makes everything happen...this love is happening for you now.

o *Meditation on Great-Great Grandmother's Dance*: Offer a guided meditation back in time, and visit your ancestor to see how she dances. What she is wearing? Where is she dancing? Envision and feel, and know the imagination of allowing.

o *Meditation on Your Name Dance*: Create a guided meditation to see yourself in a beautiful costume dancing freely in the desert. While the desert wind whispers your belly dancing name in your ear listen for it. As you let go into this calm stillness your imagination reveals all sorts of secrets. What is your name?

Learning, Natural Talents, and Practice

Learning to dance requires playing with energy. Play exposes the relationship between self-control and free abandon. Parameters are explored. Self-discipline bears the fruit of freedom. You then allow it to come to you. You even *will* it to come to you. Paramhansa Yogananda illustrates this in a description of proper prayer. He calls it "Sacred Demands." Sounds radical!

I prefer the word "demand" to "prayer" because "prayer" is based on an old-fashioned, medieval concept: God as a kingly tyrant whom we, mere subjects of His, need to supplicate and flatter...Every begging prayer, no matter how sincere, is self-limiting...we must believe that we have everything already...that is our birthright...Realize God, and you will receive everything...Be still, and let God answer you within- Paramhansa Yogananda, Whispers from Eternity

There is a strong determination in the will to dance, as well as to pray. It is easy to learn to belly dance, but hard to belly dance well! It requires a keen awareness of the senses: hearing music, seeing shapes in the mirror, kinesthetic sensitivity to rhythms and form, and an intangible harmonizing element that welcomes flow-state. It is right brained. For some, dancing is the gifted gateway to wisdom. Learning to dance can help you learn to pray. They both take will, and concentration.

What are your natural inborn gifts? What were you granted through Divine grace? How have these gifts danced you into the white veil? Use your will to unwrap them.

Seven Types of Intelligent Gifts

Psychologist Howard Gardner originally identified seven distinct types of intelligence with his Multiple Intelligences Theory in his book *Frames of Mind*. They are listed here with respect to gifted /talented children:

- *Verbal-* the ability to use words: Linguistic Children with this kind of intelligence enjoy writing, reading, telling stories or doing crossword puzzles
- *Visual-* the ability to imagine things in your mind: Spatial children think in images and pictures. They may be fascinated with mazes or jigsaw puzzles, or spend free time drawing, building with Lego's or daydreaming.
- *Physical-* the ability to use your body in various situations: Bodily-Kinesthetic kids process knowledge through bodily sensations. They are often athletic, dancers, or good at crafts such as sewing or woodworking.
- *Musical-* the ability to use and understand music: Musical children are always singing or drumming to themselves. They are usually quite aware of sounds others may miss. These kids are often discriminating listeners.
- *Mathematical-* the ability to apply logic to systems and numbers: Logical-Mathematical: Children with lots of logical intelligence are interested in patterns, categories and relationships. They are drawn to arithmetic problems, strategy games, and experiments.
- *Introspective-* the ability to understand your inner thoughts: These children may be shy. They are very aware of their own feelings, and they are self-motivated.

- *Interpersonal-* the ability to understand other people, and relate well to them: Interpersonal Children who are leaders among their peers, good at communicating, and seem to understand others' feelings and motives, possess interpersonal intelligence.

Innate abilities coded in DNA, soulful predispositions, even inherited knowledge, are all gifts of destiny. Know your spirituality by acknowledging these very gifts. They have been given as a blueprint. Work them. They embody your God-given path toward enlightenment.

What is Enlightenment?

You come to know "God" as your higher self, the Divine Spark in Judaism, Atman in Hindu, Christ-heart in Christianity, Tawhid to the Sufi, Buddha Nature to the Buddhist; all through your Divine gifts. Spirituality is revealed in the practice of self-expression, which by its very nature, holds moments of stillness and reductionism which contain the Divine.

Antithetical to the "Age of Enlightenment," an eighteenth century phenomenon in Western culture that praised reason and philosophy over what was perceived as superstition, "spiritual enlightenment" has another definition. It goes beyond rationalism.

Although the influential thinkers of the time were combating dogma and the dark ages, as they paved the way toward scientific and industrial advances, they left behind some spiritual dimension. I sometimes wonder if early indigenous people, who lived closer to nature, had a more intimate contact with the mystical. Once reason helped humanity control nature, a kind of superiority crept into the equation. It presumed that reason answered all.

Enlightenment begs to be perceived beyond intellect to include faith. It presupposes layers of "reality" not so easily seen or measured. It embraces mystery—not just mastery. Many cultures speak of enlightenment as "being in the light of God," envisioning some divine message, or experiencing revelation. Sometimes it is acknowledged as a *lightness of being* into the vastness of bliss. Whatever the experience, whether it lasts a split second or a lifetime, it is sure to alter belief.

After *enlightenment*, all things are changed. Through the practice of removing the veils, or any practice you deem appropriate to your soul, you take the journey. If nothing else, you will be kinder. It is not a goal. It is a willful wish to be open—to receive the wondrous!

Distilled to the Essential

What is essential? At art shows depicting the major works of any artist, over the span of their lifetime, emerging themes become succinct. For example, if the painter featured elaborate and lavish depictions of the horizon, their last painting, done at, say, age 90, becomes a canvas with just a horizontal line. The message distills. You become distilled into your essential self over time. You become your quintessential work of art.

Think of choreographer Jerome Robbins and his dances from West Side Story, do snapping fingers come to mind? Isadora Duncan conjures up images of flowing Grecian dresses, Fred Astaire, a top hat and cane, while Gene Kelly might remind you of singing and dancing in puddles of rain. A rose and skull can make you think of Georgia O'Keefe.

Concise mental images evoke whole scenarios, as art imitates life. That snap in West Side Story captures an attitude. Top hat and cane grant immediate debonair status, and who has not desired to splash in Gene Kelly's universal freedom puddles? The microcosm and macrocosm meet in art. Whether you zoom in or out, the vastness of space is present. You become transported by the metaphor.

What is the iconic image of you? What portrayal is your distilled legacy? What does the image say? In similar fashion, your union with Divine presence becomes distilled into the simple gesture. This makes the secular sacred. How do you find this? Could it be by holding still?

As an iconic-imaged belly dancer, I am surrounded by the swirl of Seven Veils. When I stop and sense the legacy, I see that I have handed this dance down to emerging Goddesses and Divas, all exploring an ancient feminine path to the Divine. It is a path that stretches and lifts to higher realms, to your daughter's daughters, and to your mother's mother, and right back to you again.

Clouds

A series of puffy white clouds go by, not ominous, but fluffy and friendly. Then a hand reaches out from within the clouds and holds the top of a headless dancer, twirling her.

That's how the poster looked. I was fascinated by it. How could the artist know so intimately just how I felt? That the hand of God was reaching down and dancing "me!"

When dancing, your body, mind, and soul make decisions together: artistic decisions, practical decisions, and irrational decisions. All the while, the dance goes on. The pause becomes part of it, waiting, as the ever-present hand from the cloud directs and twines you.

The dancer is headless because thought is replaced by yielding. If not, something fumbles and loses its connection with harmony. To be in harmony is to be with *what is*, and to remain open to receiving it. Ultimately, this willful letting-go opens to the hand that spins you, and you find what you need.

The Edge

I am writing to you from the edge of the earth. Really. But that could be anywhere you say. Yes, and here where sky meets sea, and sand meets me, I stand in awe. I like to be the center, but I am frequently at the edge, like many of you, because my thoughts gravitate toward the periphery. Change starts that way. Ideas, like ships peering over the horizon, bring treasures yet unknown. If you think on the edge you are able to question the norm, try new ideas on for size, and throw off the weight of the flat earth. You go in search of the curves, the space-time curves, the dancing curves, and the non-linear thinking curves.

Descartes said *"I think, therefore I am."* Could it be *"I feel, therefore I am?"* or, *"I dance, therefore I am?"* Is reality malleable? Is it dependent upon your thoughts? Perhaps you co-coordinate with the Divine energy. Perhaps you just surrender to Divine will.

There is no place that is not God. Call it what you will: God, Energy, the Universe, Life Force, Strings, Waves/Particles, you are one with it. One with all that is, always was, and always will be. The unnamable, luminous, generous giver remains constant.

Insights are the very tenets of our mystical religions, ancient philosophies, secret dance ceremonies, and modern scientific discoveries. Connections are everywhere, from past to future, East to West, and even into parallel universes. As you dance with the white veil, paradox unites. Grey areas shimmer and attract your attention more than black and white. Simple becomes an explanation for the complex. And all things are reduced to shimmering love. So how do you learn to love? You learn to love by first noticing when you are not being loving.

> *When we define ourselves, unfortunately—because we're so unkind to ourselves, we're so merciless—we forget that this grasping of the mind is just a given, and that mercy is called for. As mercy gets called forward, it makes you see what you aren't. I mean, really learning loving-kindness comes from watching how unloving we are sometimes...Love is not what we become but who we already are.* -Stephen Levine (Interview with Tami Simon, Sounds True)

If you have ever had a numinous experience of Godly love, you are never quite able to find the words to explain it. However inexpressible, it is more real than reality. You are in absolute awe. This can happen through the 7 Veils, and any other path of illumination. All the paths lead there when you remain present.

After my holy meditation experience where I was *in the light of God,* my whole life changed. After that I fell in love, got married, produced a guided meditation, and became a healer. I still struggled with learning to love. Yet all was changed. The love *in* my life changed:

We sit across the table at a fancy restaurant. The waiter brings a tall candle and lights it for us. The music of Frank Sinatra wafts through the quiet background noises of clinking crystal glasses, and forks placed on fancy plates. I gaze at my husband and see the love in his eyes. He reaches across the table and we hold hands. The loving gesture says it all, still, he speaks kind and loving invitations. Life is not particularly easy, yet it is filled with kindness. I am so lucky to love and be loved. It is miraculous to behold, and even more amazing to share it.

My reverie breaks as sea breezes caress my skin. Love leads to poetry where linear stops. I remember being in that love-light. Euphemisms abound, yet its true essence remains ephemeral. That gives you all the more reason to come to know it. You are love, you are born of love, made of love, and you live in love. I would like to say it like this:

"I love, therefore I am."

Whether learning to dance or learning to love, surrendering to practice generates mastery. Introspection births receptivity. You may ask yourself a litany of questions. "Can I do this better?" "Is this my truest expression, and is it my highest truth?" Finally you realize, it isn't coming from you! You are opening to inspiration. This happens in dance, on a non-verbal level, over and over again. There is a quintessential striving toward a Godly experience, until you are not striving at all. You are just being—just being in Divine inspiration. Just being in love and awe.

Music And

Music helps you receive. It changes the mood of your world. My mother used to say that whenever she was in a bad mood, she would put on music and it would change her outlook. I walked into her kitchen in Florida one day, while she was cooking. She was known to cook five course meals if she knew you were coming! She was in her eighties, and there she was rockin' it out, and singing along to James Brown's *I Feel Good*. I loved it! It remains a sweet memory that makes me smile.

Perhaps music is an attempt to unify the chaotic. It finds underlying patterns, real or imagined that create harmony. It connects you to others, as it bridges the mundane and sacred. In Greek, the word *music* is derived from the "the art of the Muses." It is a mathematical yet lyrical interpretation of the pulse of the universe.

You and loved ones feel separated by time and space. My son lives in Hawaii, my stepdaughter in Maine, and my granddaughter with her parents! After I watch her I see remnants of our time together, a doll here, and a book there, a plate left on the table. They are all reminders of our cherished time in sync, the old and the young who understand time better than busier people. Not that children aren't busy today, with this lesson and that practice, but children are masters at being in the moment. Their presence, if you pay attention, is like music. Drawing you into a new rhythm, the harmony where youth lives contains an "innocence" poets like to call *wasted on the young*. It is not wasted! They know how to savor the significant. If you get into their world the music is so sweet. You may forget yourself completely, and revel in the precious touch of little fingers against wrinkled skin, a past and present encounter creating a continuum of never-ending. The best music captures this engagement. Every great composer knows the pauses and rests where time seems to wait.

And, music makes you dance. Music makes you pause. Music makes you praise. Dancing to music is like meeting a person you have missed. The connection shakes you, heals you, sometimes shocks you, rocks you, and if you choose to awaken all your bodily sensate impulses, your entire being is activated, realized, and opened. You are doing the prayer-body-dance. All sound is music. All movement is dance. Where they touch is eternity. Where you truly live.

Meredith Zelman Narissi M.S., P.T.P.

At the Still Point

"Stillness"

"Be still and know that I am God"- Psalm 46

At the Still Point of the Turning World
by T.S. Eliot

At the still point of the turning world. Neither flesh nor fleshless;
Neither from nor towards; at the still point, there the dance is,
But neither arrest nor movement. And do not call it fixity,
Where past and future are gathered. Neither
movement from nor towards,
Neither ascent nor decline. Except for the point, the still point,
There would be no dance, and there is only
the dance. - *The Four Quartets*

Movement without pause is not dance. One of the hardest challenges for a new dancer is restraint. She wants to prove to you that she can do it all, and right away! She wants to show off her prowess and let you see

180

every trick in the book. Every little flourish is cherished and explored. The exuberance is non-stop, and unstoppable! It is as if nothing wants to be wasted, and giving it all at once is the best path of delight. Yet over time you learn this is not so.

The movement becomes more interesting after a pause. Holding still is fascinating. Expectation offers time for reflection. Harmony holding still is a place where there is no time, which is true.

I've seen this so often. The new dancer seems afraid to stop, like something would be ruined or lost. Moderation is missing. When I was a young dancer working in a popular night club, and very proud of my abilities, the guest dancer that night was my very own teacher, Dahlena. I was enthralled when she performed. What stunned me most was not her beauty, her costume, or even her talent. It was instead how she used it. The precision and execution of her moves were articulated with "wisdom." She played among the rhythms. They did not control her. She could pause, leaving her audience breathless in the still point.

Stillness is powerful. You feel the effects of a symphony when it is over. You see the sun setting and the light now gone. You allow for silence after a deafening applause, and perhaps you experience the space between the last breath you utter and your final transformation, as liberation.

Death of a Dance

After rehearsals that take months and months of practice, the show is over in a matter of minutes. You are at the glory, the reverb, and then, the death of a dance.

You bask in the sun's warmth after a swim in the ocean. You quench your thirst after a long run. You fall into sweet reverie after great sex. As the energy wanes, you discover impermanence. The dance is never to be done again. Not exactly like that. You are reminded of an elaborate Tibetan Buddhist sand-mandala blowing away in the wind.

How many dances have I done? Who has caught the vision before the mirage vanished? How many dances come to fruition and then like lives of passing loved ones, leave only photographic memories in sepia tones?

This passing-on brings renewal. There are new dancers, and new dances...not yours. What gets laid to rest leads to peace. The shimmer of matter returns to spirit, no more impulse to breathe, or to dance. The dance is renewed by someone else. What is the dance of the soul, when there is no body or mind to contain it? Ah, now that is some choreography!

I am reminded of being with my mother when she took her last breath.

My Story in the White Veil: On Being with the Last Breath

Vigil: sitting, standing, pacing, giggling, crying, feeling frustrated, feeling deeply peaceful, prayerful, patient and impatient...all passes through us. We are around my mother's death bed.

The sound of her death-rattle breath reminds me of a fish tank filter, maybe an old fashioned coffee pot percolating, or more precisely an American Indian Shaman's rattle. It goes on for hours.

We tell her things of this world: how much we love her, thank her, bless her, and then we begin to tell her it's ok to go...go to the light... go...go.

Then we say nothing. Beautiful mother, stroking her long black and grey hair— the first silken hair I used to cling to with my little baby hands.

After a while her face and "third eye" are peaceful, no line, just quiet breath keeps going on, like a reflex. The reverse of the developed brain. Her chest rises and falls. The breaths are subtle.

Finally her small shoulders lift slightly with the inhalation. There are only a few intakes left. I'm praying for the last breath to come, to free her, to guide her, to take her.

Then it comes. Stillness, quiet, a breeze from the window passes, and my sister's wail fills the air with loss. My mother is free.

We are left to love each other, my brothers, sister, and I...and all of us.

Dance is ultimately a Godly pursuit

Dance is ultimately a Godly pursuit. It is born of the body, like you are, yet it plays with the mind to release the soul. The body travels with you and struggles against its earth-bound chains. Gravity loves you, yet soon you long for freedom.

I marvel at how much time I have actually spent in one spot in front of a class, in a mirrored studio, any studio, feeling like I had transversed miles. It is a one-spot freedom tour, unbounded and liberated, taken mostly through the conduit of my imagination. Reminiscent of a writer sitting still, who travels through time and space, as an epic novel races past centuries onto the page.

Desire to create emerges from spirit naturally. You are born in the "image" of your creator, which means you create. Every word you speak, every thought you hold, every action you take, helps create the artwork of your life. And, it ultimately has an effect on everyone else on the planet! Through your design, you open to letting the Divine force flow. The light of eternal truth brings inspiration. You relinquish control, thereby allowing yourself to receive.

> *"What am I, what power do I have to effect anything in the world via my lowly actions? Truthfully, one should understand and know and fix in his heart/mind's thoughts, that every detail of his actions, speech and thoughts, in each instant and moment are not for naught (heaven forefend). And how many are his actions and how great and exalted, that each one rises according to it root, to effect its results in the loftiest heights, in the worlds and highest levels of the heavenly lights."* - Rav Chayyim of Volozhin, *The Soul of Life*

Abra Kedabra

Abra Kedabra! As a child you may have said these words to conjure up some fantastic magic. Maybe you wanted to make a wish come true, or to put a spell on someone...or some-thing. Did you know that aside from fairy tales and Walt Disney movies, these magic words have a history?

They come from an ancient language called Aramaic. The Aramaic alphabet was derived from the Phoenician alphabet around the 7th or 8th Century BC. It developed into a number of new languages, including Hebrew, Mongolian, Arabic, Old Turkish, and more. It was probably spoken by many belly dancers! Classical Aramaic was the main language of the Persian, Babylonian and Assyrian empires and it spread as far as Greece and the Indus valley. Accordingly, Jews, including Jesus Christ spoke an Aramaic dialect.

> *In Aramic, (Aramaic)..."Abra Kedabra" means:"I will create (a-bara) according to (ke) my word (dabara)."-* Rabbi David Zeller

The first known mention of these words was in the third century AD in a book called *Liber Medicinalis* by Quintus Serenus Sammonicus. He was a physician to the Roman emperor Caracalla, who prescribed that malaria sufferers wear an amulet containing the words Abra Kedabra written in the form of a triangle:

"Abracadabra! I will create according to my word."

A - B - R - A - C - A - D - A - B - R - A
A - B - R - A - C - A - D - A - B - R
A - B - R - A - C - A - D - A - B
A - B - R - A - C - A - D - A
A - B - R - A - C - A - D
A - B - R - A - C - A
A - B - R - A - C
A - B - R - A
A - B - R
A - B
A

There are many references about God speaking some-thing into existence. In Genesis it states: God said, "Let there be light, and there was light." Hindu's have a word for the sound of the universe being created: "OM." Was it first a thought, a sound, or light taking form? Sound is a vibration in the continuum of light's spectrum. If God speaks things into existence, do you, being created in his image, have some aspect of this ability?

New age spiritual books abound that assert that you can think and grow rich, create good health, change your DNA, and more precisely use speech and thought for the creation of your own life.

> *"When you ask for the manifestation prior to the vibration, you ask the impossible. When you are willing to offer the vibration before the manifestation…all things are possible. It is Law…You have to begin to tell the story of your life as you now want it to be and discontinue the tales of how it has been or how it is."* - Ester and Jerry Hicks, *The Law of Attraction*

How you speak creates situations in your life. More precisely, how you feel and speak creates much of your circumstance. This free will is often underestimated.

What if you spoke only in highest truths? If your words came only after you honored silence, that would sound like prayer.

"May the words of my mouth and the meditations of my heart be acceptable to you oh Lord, my Rock and my Redeemer -Psalm 19:14

Like the ancients, you can also *dance* your intentions into existence. You can use feeling to the maximum. Your body can reach another level of intensity. It can become a prayer-body experience. Then, how you move becomes as important as how you speak. Abra Kedabra, may it be so!

The Veil of Stillness Unveils Peace

Strangely enough, you *can* be still while you dance. Stillness is an inner state. There is a presence that exists in the mind while you are moving. The mind can listen to the heart. The body can listen to the heart too. The heart listens for Divine presence. Just as a mantra keeps the mind occupied while the meditator observes undercurrents, dance can occupy the body while the heart soars.

The energy traveling from floor to feet, and hips to heart and hands, undulates in a vast oceanic awareness of flowing love. While passing through the heart, joy is awakened on its way to peace. This peace holds the blessing of being alive. This peace brings you to the wings of the infinite One.

Prayer-Body Birthing Dance

The art of belly dance unveils your feminine essence. Dancing through the veils, you find mystical secrets of profound creativity. Hidden in this dance, you discover a literal portrayal of the process. You reenact creating life!

Elegantly, the dancer mimics birth in undulating abdominal waves. The body rocks in a watery, shimmering motion. In ancient times women belly danced to strengthen their bodies for childbirth. Today they still do. But is it not only for childbirth. Something else is trying to be born.

When birthing a baby you are asked to *be with* the development more than to cause it. When pregnant you do not think, "Now I will make the ears, the eyes, and yes, the little hands and feet." You are not doing the process. You are receiving it.

Belly dance mimics this. It celebrates this life force. You are being the birthing Goddess as you dance. You let the same cosmic intelligence present at physical conception enter you as you dance. You are honoring God's work. You become a *bringer of being*. Each undulation now imitates the bearing of faith and devotion.

You are a Divine being conceiving the Divine. You receive and conceive. If not singly, then collectively. All of us birthing a new consciousness of love.

Energy moves. Even within the stillness of a dense rock you know there are vibrating elements of nature. Stars move. You move. The child waiting to be born moves. When you move with artful intention it becomes dance. This dance moves toward the light, if you let it. It becomes your prayer-body dance. And what is this prayer but to know God?

The belly dance initiation births the God presence within you. This is the greatest mystical secret of all. It is you giving birth. *It is you giving birth to God!*

You are conceiving holiness. The conception of God becomes real in your life. It is a manifestation of your unveiled enlightenment. Cosmic love flows. You give it life by receiving it. You recognize and share it. You birth it. The great mystery of love birthing itself "pre-veils."

Holy Birth

Iconic images of holy birth abound. In story, art, and dance, since humankind began to wonder, birth legends have held fascinating implications.

Roman and Greek myths tell of humans and gods giving birth to temperamental offspring with equally human and Divine attributes. Mother and Divine-child statues are cross-culturally celebrated. From Africa to Europe, to Eastern cultures, and beyond, mother-Goddesses carry newborns with glowing emanations surrounding their heads.

Miraculous births are found in varied cultures. Barren women from the old testament, like Rachel, Sarah, and Hannah, having had their "wombs opened by God" gave birth to prominent children in Hebrew history.

Mary's immaculate conception foretells the Virgin Birth of Jesus. The birthing of Jesus is also the birth of Christianity and Christ-consciousness. It is interesting to note that the *virgin* conception, just like your own God-consciousness, is a spiritual, *not* material process. It symbolizes the holy nature of birthing God.

In Hinduism, Vishnu descends into the womb of Devaki to create the deity Krishna. One night, Queen Mayadevi dreamed that a white elephant descended from heaven and entered her womb. Soon the Buddha was born. Thereafter he took seven steps and declared his "chief" place in the world. Zoroaster's birth was also noted as miraculous, when at birth, he burst out laughing and the whole universe rejoiced with him. Some Taoist schools deem that Laozi was conceived when his mother gazed at a falling star. The ancient Aztec Quetzalcoatl, is said to have been born of a virgin, who was dreaming of the god Ometeotl, known then, as *the creator of all creation.*

These sacred stories, by metaphor and myth, are powerful truth holders. They remind you that birth is spiritual. They echo the spiritual birthing required to unveil your own sacred-self. They proclaim that you too are a holy child.

The "miraculous" woman giving birth is perhaps taken for granted. Some may perceive her status as not quite so divine. Belly dance reclaims the wonder and status of Divine woman. Not in the literal sense, but by her personal spiritual renaissance. By playing the Goddess, she becomes one. Then she recognizes that this holy nature must come out...into her life.

When retrieval of your soulful nature surfaces, it is an opportunity to heal the world. All of you, through the wondrous birthing of your own sacred-soul reclaimation, can reframe the human experience. You can receive the internal God-Goddess being born. It is being born from you. This birthing unveils the enlightenment of peace.

These are the seven veils. As you pass through the veil of denial into desire, from sensing into insight, you observe the self. You recognize the love that you are. This heals you through compassion. Then as you promise to live up to this loving-kindness, the understanding of Divine connection comes to you. Finally, you hold stillness. You hold it long enough to surrender to "the peace of God, which passeth all understanding."

You feel God, you know something of the Divine, and you give it forth, like giving birth. You know a love that can give and be given, with immense gratitude.

Dance with the veils, shed your inhibitions through one veil of discovery to the next. Each invites you, with its color and curious light, onward toward higher realms.

Unveil the sacred mysteries. Share what you have to offer. Only you can offer your gifts. The veils are portals of mystical secrets, some of which will be only yours to discover.

> *"All things are living; all things are dancing*
> *in the rhythm of eternal harmony."*
> -Paramahansa Yogananda

Come. Together we dance the luminous journey. Body awaken the spirit. Earthly realms unite in transcendent joy. Dance here on this earth. Bring "earth as it is in heaven." Raise the holy sparks. Birth Divine consciousness. Dance your dance and unveil your own mystical secrets. I encourage you to offer yours. You are the Dancing One!

You and I, let us dance together in eternal harmony and peace.
May all life dance in eternal harmony and peace.
May it be a dance of love.
May it be so.
Amen

BIBLIOGRAPHY

Clarissa Pinkola Estes, PH.D.. *Women Who Run With The Wolves: Myths and Stories of the Wild Woman Archetype.* New York, Ballantine Books, 1992

Abigail Brenner M.D. *Women's Rites of Passage: How to Embrace Change and Celebrate Life*, Rowman & Littlefield Publishers, Inc. 2007

Rita Silverman, Abigail Brenner, M.D. *Replacement Children: The Unconscious Script*, Kindle Edition, Sand Hill Review Press, 2015

Jean Shinoda Bolen, M.D. *Goddesses in Everywoman.* New York, 1984

Lama Zopa Rinpoche, *Ultimate Healing, the power of Compassion.* Massachusetts, 2001

Oscar Wilde, *Salome, A tragedy in one Act*, Kindle edition, original play 1891

Caroline Myss, PH.D. *Anatomy of the Spirit.* New York, Harmony Books, 1996

Foundation for Inner Peace, *A Course in Miracles*, third edition. California, 1975

John O'Donohue, *To Bless the Space Between Us: A Book of Blessings*, New York, Doubleday 2008

Merlin Stone, *When God Was A Woman*, New York, The Dial Press, 1976

Elizabeth Cunningham, *The Passion of Mary Magdalen: a novel*, Rhinebeck, New York, Monkfish Book Publishing Company, 2007

Joan Borysenko, Ph.D. *Pocketful of Miracles*. New York, Warner Books, 1994

Marvin W. Meyer, *The Nag Hammadi Scriptures*, Harper Collins e-books, 2013

Paramahansa Yogananda, *The Poetry of Paramahansa Yogananda*, e-books, 1939

Cia Sautter, *The Miriam Tradition: Teaching Embodied Torah*, Chicago, University of Illinois Press, 2010

Maya Angelou, *Wouldn't Take Nothing for My Journey Now*, New York, Bantam Books, 1993

Patanjali, *The Yoga Sutras of Patanjali*. Munich, Book/Rix, Amazon Digital Services, 2015

Marianne Williamson, *The Law of Divine Compensation: on work, Money, and Miracles*, New York. Harper One. 2012

Daniel C. Matt, *The Essential Kabbalah*: The heart of Jewish Mysticism, Harper Collins e-books. 1995

Elaine Aron, *The Highly Sensitive Child: Helping Our Children Thrive When the World Overwhelms Them*. United States, Harmony Books, 2015

Bruce Berger, *Esoteric Anatomy*: The Body As Consciousness, California, North Atlantic Books, 1998

John Beaulieu, N.D., Ph.D., R.P.P. *Polarity Therapy Workbook*. New York, BioSonic Enterprises, Ltd. 1994

Dr. Randolph Stone, D.C., D.O. Dr. *Randolph Stone's Polarity Therapy: The complete collected works*. CRCS Wellness Books. Tennessee 1986

Harvilel Hendrix, Ph.D. and Helen LaKelly Hunt, Ph.D. *Receiving Love: Transform Your Relationship by Letting Yourself Be Loved*, New York, Atria Books, 2004

Angeles Arrien, *The Second Half of Life*, Amazon Digital Services, Inc. 2009

Louise L. Hay, *You Can Heal Your Life*, New York, Hay House

Gregg Krech, Niakan: *Gratitude, Grace, and the Japanese Art of Self-Reflection*, Stone Bridge Press, California,2002

Richard Francis Burton, John Payne: *One Thousand and One- Complete Arabian Nights Collection*, Delphi Classics, 2015 Kindle edition

Deepak Chopra, M.D. *The Seven Spiritual Laws of Success: A practical Guide to the Fulfillment of Your Dreams*, New World Library/Amber/ Allen Publishing 1994

Deepak Chopra, M.D., *Synchrodestiny: Harnessing the Infinite Power of Coincidence to Create Miracles*, Rider & Company, 2004

Christopher Key Chapple, *Yoga and the Luminous: Pantanjali's Spiritual Path to Freedom*, SUNY Press, 2008

Geri Larkin, *Close to the Ground: Reflections on the Seven Factors of Enlightenment*, Rodmell Press, 2013

Joseph Campbell, Bill Moyers, *The Power of Myth*, Anchor, 1991

Edward Lear, *Nonsense Drolleries The Owl & The Pussy-Cat- The Duck & The Kangaroo*, Kindle edition, Amazon Digital Services LLC 2012

Kahil Gibran, *The Prophet*, Alfred A. Knopf publisher, 1923

Olive Schreiner, *Dreams (Classic Reprint)*, Forgotten Books, 2015

Carol Gilligan Ph.D, *In a Different Voice*, Harvard University Press, 1982

Gloria Steinem, *Revolution from Within: a book of Self-Esteem*, kindle edition, open Road media, 2012

Shakti Gawain, *Creative Visualization: Use the Power of Your Imagination to Create What You Want in Your Life*, New World Library, Nataraj, 2002

Stephen Levine, *Guided Meditations, Explorations ad Healings*, Kindle edition, Anchor Publishing 2010

T.S. Eliot, *Four Quartets*, Kindle Edition, Mariner Books, 2014

Rav Chayyim of Volozhin, *The Soul of Life: The Complete Neffesh Ha-Chayyim, paperback,* New Davar Publications, 2012

APPENDIX

7 Veils Chart

First	Red Veil of Denial	Unveils Desire
Second	Orange Veil of Sensation	Unveils Insight
Third	Yellow Veil of Observation	Unveils the Self
Fourth	Green Veil of Love	Unveils Compassion
Fifth	Blue Veil of Integration	Unveils Healing
Sixth	Purple Veil of Promise	Unveils Divine Connection
Seventh	White Veil of Stillness	Unveils Peace